THE IMPRINT OF MAN

edited by
Emmanuel Anati

Also in this series:

André Leroi-Gourhan
The dawn of European art: an introduction to palaeolithic cave painting

Antonio Beltrán
Rock art of the Spanish Levant

Campbell Grant
The rock art of the North American Indians

THE IMPRINT OF MAN

The rock art of southern Africa

Published by the Press Syndicate of the University of Cambridge
The Pitt Building, Trumpington Street, Cambridge CB2 1RP
32 East 57th Street, New York, NY 10022, USA
296 Beaconsfield Parade, Middle Park, Melbourne 3206, Australia

First published 1983

Printed in Italy

Library of Congress catalogue card number: 82-14642

British Library Cataloguing in Publication Data
Lewis-Williams, J. David
The rock art of Southern Africa.
—(The Imprint of man)
1. Petroglyphs—Southern Africa
I. Title II. Series
732'.23'0968   GN865.84
ISBN 0 521 24460 9

The rock art
of southern Africa

J. DAVID LEWIS-WILLIAMS

Department of Archaeology, University of the Witwatersrand, Johannesburg

CAMBRIDGE UNIVERSITY PRESS

CAMBRIDGE
LONDON   NEW YORK   NEW ROCHELLE
MELBOURNE   SYDNEY

Contents

Prologue

The kloofs or chasms, washed by torrents of water rushing down the steep sides of the high stratified mountains, frequently leave a succession of caverns, of which the Bosjesman chooses the highest, as not only removing him farther from the danger of a surprise, but giving him also the command of a greater extent of country.

In one of these retreats were discovered their recent traces. The fires were scarcely extinguished, and the grass on which they had slept was not yet withered. On the smooth sides of the cavern were drawings of several animals that had been made from time to time by these savages. Many of them were caricatures; but others were too well executed not to arrest attention. The different antelopes that were there delineated had each their character so well discriminated, that the originals, from whence the representations had been taken, could, without any difficulty, be ascertained. Among the numerous animals that were drawn, was the figure of a zebra remarkably well done; all the marks and characters of this animal were accurately represented – and the proportions were seemingly correct. The force and spirit of drawings, given to them by bold touches judiciously applied, and by the effect of light and shadow, could not be expected from savages; but for accuracy of outline and correctness of the different parts, worse drawings than that of the zebra have passed through the engraver's hands. The materials with which they had been executed were charcoal, pipe-clay, and the different ochres. The animals represented were zebras, qua-chas, gemsboks, springboks, reeboks, elands, baboons, and ostriches, all of which, except the gemsbok, are found upon the very spot. Several crosses, circles, points, and lines, were placed in a long rank as if intended to express some meaning; but no other attempt appeared at the representation of inanimate objects. In the course of travelling, I had frequently heard the peasantry mention the drawings in the mountains behind the Sneuwberg made by the Bosjesmans; but I took it for granted they were caricatures only, similar to those on the doors and walls of uninhabited buildings, the works of idle boys; and it was no disagreeable disappointment to find them very much the reverse. Some of the drawings were known to be new; but many of them had been remembered from the first settlement of this part of the Colony.

Sir John Barrow
*An Account of Travels into the Interior of Southern Africa
in the Years 1797 and 1798*
Volume I, pages 239–40

1 Twyfelfontein
2 Brandberg
3 Tsodilo Hills
4 Nswatugi
5 Silozwane
6 Lion's Head
7 Diana's Vow
8 Apollo 11
9 Danielskuil
10 Wonderwerk
11 Vlakplaas
12 Kinderdam
13 Doornhoek
14 Bothaville
15 Orkney
16 Eland's Bay
17 Hex River
18 Springbok Oog
19 Leeuwfontein
20 Buffelsfontein
21 De Rust
22 Barkly East
23 Cala
24 Orange Springs; Tripolitania
25 Ha Khotso
26 Manamolela
27 Leqoa River
28 Hermitage
29 Sehonghong
30 Giant's Castle
31 Marten's Shelter; Ndedema Gorge
32 Mushroom Hill
33 Boomplaas
34 Coldstream

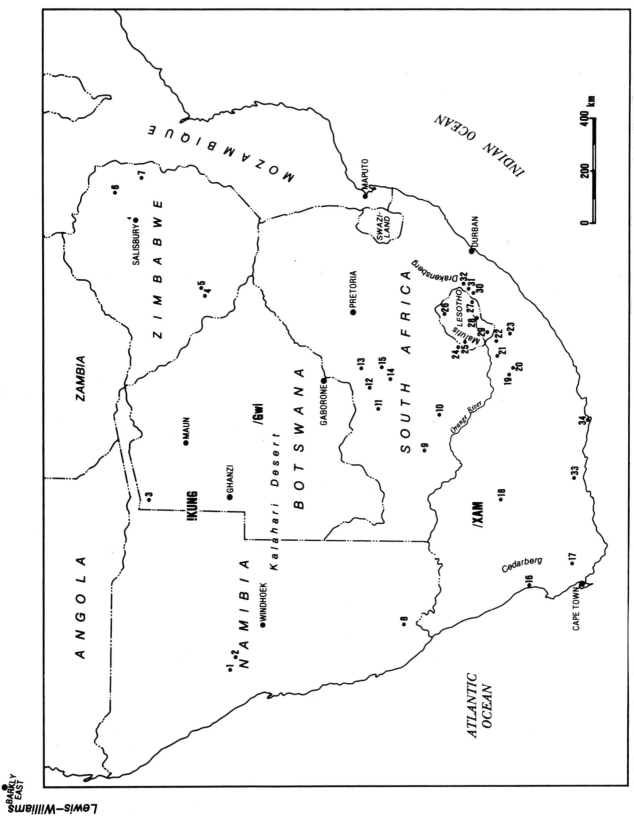

1 Map of southern Africa showing places and Bushman groups mentioned in the text.

CHAPTER ONE

Perspectives

The Prologue to this book is taken from Sir John Barrow's account of a journey he undertook in 1797 and 1798 into the then largely unknown interior of southern Africa. In this extract he expresses his surprise and delight at coming upon a rock shelter filled with paintings 'too well executed not to arrest attention'. His discovery was made after an arduous journey by ox-wagon across sweltering plains and over precipitous mountains. But he considered the privations of travel in those early days worthwhile because the rock art he found suggested that the Bushmen, a race long despised and ill-treated by the white settlers, were not as barbaric as he had been led to believe. The excellent draughtsmanship and sense of movement given to the paintings by those untutored artists could not, he wrote, 'be expected from savages'. He had been told about paintings hidden in the mountains, but those he found far exceeded his expectations and confirmed his view that the Bushmen had been rendered more worthy of the 'name savage . . . by the conduct of the European settlers'. Barrow was not the first white traveller to see Bushman rock art, but he was one of the first to appreciate both its extraordinary aesthetic worth and its significance for a more realistic assessment of the much maligned Bushmen.

Barrow made his illuminating discovery in 1797. Today it is still possible in some parts of southern Africa to climb the remote 'kloofs or chasms, washed by torrents of water' until one reaches a rock shelter unvisited since the last Bushmen left over a century ago. Stone artefacts lie on the floor as they were abandoned, and on the walls are some of the most breath-taking examples of so-called 'primitive' art in the world. Barrow's enthusiastic response was entirely appropriate: the minute detail, delicate shading and lively compositions still captivate visitors to these astonishing natural galleries. Further inland from the mountains there are far fewer rock shelters suitable for habitation or art. Here countless rock engravings (petroglyphs) have been chipped or incised into flat rocks on the hill-tops and next to streams. The engravings, though less well-known than the paintings, are in no way inferior; as the illustrations in this book show, some are as splendid as the best paintings. 'Primitive' art sometimes appears grotesque or naive to insensitive westerners who have preconceived and rigid notions about what 'art' should look like, but Bushman paintings and engravings make an immediate appeal to all.

It is not only the obvious aesthetic excellence of the art which is so striking; the sheer quantity

7

9, 11, 35–7,
106–8

of the work is, perhaps, even more amazing. No one knows just how many art sites, paintings and engravings, there are. The number of recorded sites grows each year. By 1981 the locations of 3931 sites had been noted by the Archaeological Data Recording Centre in Cape Town, and this impressive total excludes the numerous richly painted sites in Zimbabwe, Namibia, Botswana, Lesotho, Swaziland and Moçambique, as well as many more in South Africa which are known but not yet reported. Recently Aron Mazel's survey of only certain parts of the Natal Drakensberg raised the number of known sites there from 396 to 516, while Lucas Smits estimates the number of sites in Lesotho at 5000; on the eastern slopes of the Natal Drakensberg alone there are more than 29 800 individual paintings. It is not surprising that southern Africa has been called 'the richest storehouse of prehistoric art in the world'. It is difficult to know if this extravagant claim is justified; very probably it is. Certainly, anyone who has studied the far more limited Palaeolithic art of western Europe is overwhelmed by the abundance of Bushman art. The discovery of a new painted site in Europe is an exciting event; in southern Africa it is almost an everyday occurrence.

The southern African rock art differs in a number of other ways from the perhaps better known Palaeolithic art of Lascaux, Altimira and other celebrated sites in western Europe. Much, but by no means all, the European art is concealed in deep underground caverns; frequently one has to crawl, climb and even swim for considerable distances before reaching the subterranean art. The southern African rock shelters, on the other hand, are all open: the sun often shines directly onto the paintings. Furthermore, the southern African paintings are generally smaller than the European paintings. It is rare to find a painting that is in any way comparable with the large bulls of Lascaux, or the imposing horses of Pech-Merle. Some of the exquisite Bushman masterpieces are only a few centimetres long, yet they show amazing attention to detail.

Another significant difference between the two arts should also be noted. So-called narrative scenes are rare in the European art and are accordingly much publicised. The well-known example in the shaft at Lascaux seems to show a man being gored by a wounded bison, yet writers have proposed numerous ingenious, if contradictory, explanations. In southern Africa similarly narrative compositions are far more common and much more explicit: people are clearly depicted dancing, fighting, hunting or performing the ritual activities I describe in subsequent chapters.

The explicitness of so many such groups in the southern African art is one of the factors which seem to make its understanding a more promising enterprise than the interpretation of the enigmatic European art. The dark, numinous caverns of Europe readily suggest an arcane, religious motive, but in southern Africa the apparently clear narrative scenes together with the sunny, open rock shelters and the abundance of the art point to something simpler and less esoteric. Bushman art has therefore never lacked interpreters, but, as I show in this book, many have been misled into believing the depictions to be far less complex than they actually are.

Understanding what rock art meant to its original viewers is indeed the ultimate goal of most writers whether they are concerned with the European Palaeolithic art, the Australian Aborigine paintings or the prolific engravings of Alpine Valcamonica. Yet all too often their interpretations clearly reflect their own milieu rather than that of the artists. It is very difficult to rid oneself of the preconceived ideas of one's own culture. Despite claims to the contrary, there is no reason to suppose that the Palaeolithic artists of twenty thousand years ago, or, for that matter, the Bushman artists of one hundred and more years ago, were moved by the same interests as present-day western artists. When the artists have been dead for so long and came from so different a

11

culture, a reconstruction of their motives and cognitive system is fraught with almost insuperable problems.

Nevertheless, it is with that sanguine expectation that I write this book on Bushman art: my ultimate aim is to furnish some understanding of what the Bushman artists were communicating or accomplishing when they painted in their rock shelters. This seemingly impossible task is made considerably easier by a record of Bushman life and thought which was compiled in the 1870s and is thus contemporary with the last artists. This extensive ethnography preserves many myths and beliefs of the now extinct southern Bushmen, as well as accounts of their life style, and at once sets the southern African art apart from the European. In Europe we know nothing about the artists' religion; everything must be inferred from the art itself or from often ambiguous archaeological contexts. But in southern Africa we have a good idea of the artists' beliefs, and we can use these to understand the paintings.

The nineteenth-century record shows that the art was an integral and important part of Bushman culture. I therefore start by describing, albeit briefly, the Bushman economy, social structure and religion. This description provides an indispensable background because the art cannot be interpreted outside of its social and conceptual context. I then outline the distribution of the paintings in time and space to show that we are dealing with a single artistic expression and not with the work of disparate peoples and epochs. This temporal and spatial uniformity means that at least some of the nineteenth-century ethnography is probably applicable far from the homes of the early informants. Indeed, many of the most important concepts and beliefs still persist among the Bushman groups which survive in the Kalahari Desert.

Meticulous research is necessary to isolate features of the art which reflect those explanatory concepts. I therefore describe in Chapter Four some of the techniques currently used in southern Africa to study the art. We can now see just which subjects the artists chose to emphasise and which they tended to ignore. The fifth chapter goes on to argue that many prominent features of the art depict some of the key metaphors which gave form and meaning to the Bushmen's ideas about the cosmos and their place in it. An understanding of how these metaphors worked enables us to 'read' otherwise enigmatic paintings. So the sixth chapter of this book is an explanation of some complex paintings which, without detailed knowledge of Bushman life and thought, would remain for ever intriguing and baffling.

Barrow and many other writers since have assumed that the art was no more than a remarkable exercise in aesthetics. On the contrary, much of the art was associated with beliefs and metaphors which underpinned the Bushman cognitive system. The importance of the art to the artists and their contemporaries can therefore hardly be overestimated.

CHAPTER TWO

Hunters and artists

Sir John Barrow was one of the more enlightened travellers in southern Africa. Despite the persuasive artistic evidence, many others could find no redeeming features in the Bushmen. As long ago as 1731 Kolben described them as 'Troops of abandon'd Wretches who . . . sally out from Time to Time into the fields to steal cattle for their Sustenance'. The missionaries frequently despaired of bringing such 'wild' Bushmen into the Christian fold. One frustrated missionary declared comprehensively: 'He has no religion, no laws, no government, no recognised authority, no patrimony, no fixed abode . . . a soul, debased, it is true, and completely bound down and clogged by his animal nature.'

The people had been named 'Bosjesmans' by the Dutch colonists because, some said, of their deplorable practice of cunningly concealing themselves in the bushes before springing out on the unwary traveller. More recently, writers have understandably felt that 'Bushman' is pejorative and they therefore prefer 'San', the Khoikhoi or Hottentot name for the hunters who belong to several language groups and thus do not themselves have a single name to cover all the groups. In many ways 'San' does seem preferable, but even that word was probably denigratory in the Hottentot language. Because this book is intended for a general readership, I retain the traditional 'Bushman' without, it will soon become plain, any of the adverse connotations the word had in Barrow's time and which, for some people, it most unfortunately retains nearly two hundred years later.

1   Today virtually none of these misunderstood southern Bushmen remain. The only Bushmen who survive are those who live further to the north in the less hospitable Kalahari Desert. In recent decades the various Kalahari groups, such as the !Kung, have been much studied by anthropologists and have, in fact, become one of the best understood hunter–gatherer societies. Contrary to popular belief, these modern people are not the fugitive descendants of southern painters who were driven into the desert by the advance of white and black farmers. They belong to distinct linguistic groups; at the end of the nineteenth century their language was altogether unintelligible to the last southern Bushmen. Furthermore, their fine adjustment to desert life suggests that they have lived in the Kalahari for a very long time, and this is confirmed by archaeological evidence. The flat, sandy desert offers few places for them to paint or engrave, so it

13

is not surprising that they have no tradition of rock art. Some !Kung Bushmen do, however, know of paintings in the Tsodilo Hills in north-west Botswana, but they deny that they were done by Bushmen; they say God put the paintings there. Only if pressed on this point will they concede that the Tsaukwe Bushmen, a group away to the south-west, could have painted the pictures. They think the paintings are beautiful, but they have little to say about them. Despite these and other differences between the Kalahari Bushmen and the extinct southern Bushmen, research has shown that it is legitimate to draw on the more recent source of information in those areas of belief where specific and detailed connections between it and the nineteenth-century southern ethnography can be shown. There is now sufficient reason to believe that the extinct southern painters had a cognitive system very similar to (but not identical with) that still preserved in parts of the Kalahari.

Nevertheless, I depend principally on the older material because it is contemporary with the

2 Below, left: A /Gwi hunter in the Kalahari. Note his link-shaft arrow. Below, right: !Kung Bushmen preparing the skin of a large antelope which they have pegged out on the ground. A woman with a baby on her back walks past them. In the background to the right is a heavily thatched summer (wet season) shelter; outside lie two ostrich eggshells which are used for storing water. Top: /Gwi Bushmen skinning a gemsbok. Large kills like this are today comparatively rare occurrences.

last artists and so more directly relevant to the paintings. The opportunity to compile such a record of Bushman life and belief would have been lost for ever were it not for a few far-sighted people who realised that an entire way of life and a whole language were disappearing. One of these was the German linguist Wilhelm Bleek, who compiled the Bushman ethnography to which I referred in the last chapter. He was chiefly interested in the various languages spoken by Bushmen and Hottentot groups, and it was he who discovered that there were in fact a number of Bushman language 'families' which were mutually unintelligible. His research received a considerable boost in 1870 when he learned that some /Xam Bushmen had been brought to Cape Town as convicts to work on the construction of a new breakwater in Table Bay. These unfortunate men had been convicted of such crimes as sheep stealing. Bleek, moved by their plight, persuaded the Governor to allow some of the Bushmen to live with him in his suburban home. The friendship which grew up between the Bleek family and their informants was so great that, when their term of penal servitude expired, some chose to remain in Cape Town, and some even brought their families to assist in teaching their very difficult Bushman language. To facilitate his work Bleek developed a phonetic script in which he and his sister-in-law, Lucy Lloyd, took down over twelve thousand pages of verbatim text. By any standards this was a formidable achievement. In those thousands of pages 'Stone Age' Bushmen speak directly to the modern researcher about their way of life, rituals, myths and beliefs.

1   The region from which Bleek's nineteenth-century /Xam Bushmen came is semi-arid. The people had therefore to live in small groups comprising only a few extended families. Early reports suggest that these groups numbered eight to twelve members or twenty to twenty-five members; some larger groups of seventy or even a hundred were reported, but these were exceptional and might have resulted from several groups being forced to unite in opposition to the white farmers' advance. In the south-western Cape there is a distinctive type of painting which
3 shows seated figures wearing skin cloaks; they are so close together that their bodies seem to merge. A study of these and other paintings has shown that the artists might have distinguished

3 A group of seated human figures. They are so close together that their bodies seem to merge. Above them is a line of bags and other equipment probably suspended from the wall or ceiling of a rock shelter. Colour: red. Cedarberg, south-western Cape.

between the two smaller group sizes. Elsewhere, however, it has not been possible to relate the size of Bushman groups to the numbers of people depicted together in the paintings.

In discussions of the Bushmen it has long been customary to refer to these groups as 'bands', but I follow Richard Lee, who has studied the Kalahari !Kung Bushmen, in preferring 'camp'. 'Band' is associated with the idea of a closely knit group related in the male line and defending a clearly defined territory, but the structure of a Bushman camp is much more fluid than this. The southern Bushman /Xam camp had as its nucleus a few married brothers and sisters with, perhaps, their father. Amongst the Kalahari !Kung, whose camps are similarly structured, the name of one of the related older people may become associated with the camp. This person is not, however a chief or headman in the generally accepted sense of those words: he does not exercise any special privileges. The southern /Xam language, indeed, had no word for 'chief': Bushman society was and still is essentially egalitarian.

Being under no authority, members of a camp were free to come and go as they wished. Numerous tales recorded by Wilhelm Bleek mention the frequent visiting which kept up a constant circulation of population between camps. People could decide to live with any camp in which there was a related person no matter how remote the relationship. Furthermore, it is possible that the southern Bushmen, like the modern !Kung Bushmen, could have claimed relationship simply on the grounds that someone had the same name as oneself or the name of a close relative. In the Kalahari today a man can claim residence in a camp because someone in that camp has the same name as, say, his brother; that person is seen as a second brother.

All people in a /Xam camp, whether established residents or visitors, had access to two or more
2 waterholes which, in some cases, might also have been shared with another camp. Their flimsy shelters were built some distance from the water so that they would not frighten off the animals which came to drink there. Two of these waterholes formed the focus of summer and winter residence; when one hole dried up or turned bitter, the camp moved to another. Accounts of these movements suggest that at least a two-day march separated waterholes. The people had, therefore, to spend one or more nights on the way and had to carry water in ostrich eggshells. The unpredictable and highly localised rainfall was another factor governing movements. Bleek's informants spoke of moving to patches of plant food which sprang up after localised summer thunderstorms; in the winter they were dependent upon bulbs and moved to areas known to support plants of this type.

Further to the east, in the better watered and more mountainous regions, rainfall similarly governed the seasonal movement of Bushman camps. A study of climatic and vegetational zones has shown that several camps probably amalgamated during the period from September to the
1, 57, 69 end of January and moved to the higher areas of the Drakensberg mountain where many of the painted shelters are found. The summer rains of this time cause the new, sweet grass to spring up, and this attracts herds of migratory antelope. In the cold winter months the grass turns sour and plant foods are scarce; at this more difficult time the Bushman camps probably split up and descended to the less harsh lower regions where there are far fewer rock paintings.

This shifting and seasonally controlled economy was based on hunting and gathering: the men hunted a variety of animals while the women gathered plant food. From the earliest reports onwards writers have been impressed, even astounded, by the Bushmen's tracking and hunting abilities. The hoofprints of a wounded animal can be detected amongst the confused tracks of a

4 In the upper part of this lively group men are working on a small antelope skin which they have pegged out on the ground. Compare this painting with the photograph (2) of !Kung men performing the same task. Scale in centimetres. Fergie's Cave, Giant's Castle, Natal Drakensberg.

whole herd; they are then followed until the failing animal leaves the herd and is eventually found dead. The Bushman interest in animal tracks is reflected in the art; in both engravings and paintings there are distinctive hoofprints. So accurately drawn are these tracks that Kalahari Bushmen were able to identify some in a copy of a Drakensberg painting as quite definitely of eland.

Although Bushmen do a fair amount of trapping, the most esteemed method of hunting is with
5 bow and arrow. The Bushman link-shaft arrow was, and in the Kalahari still is, a complex piece of equipment comprising four parts. In former times the point was made of stone or bone, but since contact with the iron-smelting Bantu-speaking farmers the Bushmen have also used triangular iron points. The point is fixed to a short reed collar which is, in turn, connected to the main shaft of the arrow by a small torpedo-shaped piece of wood or bone, the so-called 'link'. When the arrow strikes an animal, the impact causes this link to split the shaft so that the longer portion falls away and the point is left embedded in the animal. Neither rubbing against a tree, nor the
19 movements of running can then easily dislodge the point. Numerous paintings accurately depict
25 such arrows. They are finely painted in sections of red and white to indicate the various parts; some even distinguish between the slender bone points and the broader iron points. Sometimes the arrows are shown held by a hunter. In other paintings they are lodged between the hunter's
89 back and his short skin cloak, or else fixed in a 'crown' around the head. Both positions facilitated rapid discharge of arrows; it is easier to seize an arrow from one of these positions than to extract it from the narrow opening of a quiver.

Animals do not succumb at once to the puny Bushman arrows; it is the deadly poison which eventually causes their death. In a few paintings there is a very small red dot just behind the point. This may represent the poison which we know was placed there to avoid blunting the point in any way. Today the Kalahari Bushmen make their poison from the larvae of a small beetle, but the southern Bushmen seem to have used a variety of poisons which they made from plants, especially the euphorbia, and snake venom. The poison is very dangerous and is greatly feared by the Bushmen themselves; the bone points are therefore kept reversed so that the poison is safely contained within the reed collar. The poisoned arrow has, in fact, been called the 'nuclear deterrent' of the Bushmen. If men argue violently, the women rush to hide their arrows; death

5   A modern !Kung link-shaft arrow which is so constructed that, on impact, the shaft falls away and the poisoned point remains in the animal.

must inevitably follow a wound. Even a large antelope like an eland will succumb if only a small quantity enters its bloodstream. The poison is cardiotoxic and does not contaminate the whole animal. The spot where the arrow struck is cut out and thrown away, but the rest of the meat is fit to eat. The effect of the poison is, however, not instantaneous and the hunters have to track the animal, perhaps for a few days. This delay means that the hunters are sometimes forestalled by vultures and other scavengers which consume the carcass; disappointment is sometimes the only reward for days of arduous tracking in the burning Kalahari sun.

To compensate for the essentially chancy nature of such hunting and to ensure an adequate supply of protein the Bushmen observe strict rules relating to the sharing of meat. Early writers frequently commended the generous sharing of meat which followed the successful shooting and tracking of an antelope among the southern Bushmen, and more detailed accounts of the rules governing sharing have been recorded for the modern Kalahari Bushmen. The meat is distributed according to kinship ties and even by the name-relationships to which I have referred. No one in a camp goes without a portion.

The plant food collected by a woman, on the other hand, is consumed by her family only. To obtain edible roots the southern Bushwomen used a digging stick weighted with a stone. These stones, the size of a fist and larger, were laboriously bored through and then fixed to the stick with wedges. Some women are shown in the art with weighted digging sticks, but they do not appear frequently. In the southern Drakensberg only eighty-six women were identified amongst 4530 human figures. The paucity of paintings of women is perhaps surprising, because they made a substantial contribution to the economy. In the Kalahari the women supply over 60% of the camp's food. The artists were evidently principally concerned with matters other than the provision of food.

Even in a society like this in which food was shared and all people were equal, tensions arose from time to time. Some tensions were social, others were 'ecological'. The social tensions resulted mainly from the ambivalent position of people who married into the camp, from disputed marriage arrangements and from disagreements over the equitable distribution of meat. The 'ecological' tensions, on the other hand, arose from the comparatively fickle environment: game, rain and plant foods were unpredictable resources believed to be under the control of supernatural powers and beings. Three overlapping categories of medicine men concerned themselves with these social and ecological problems.

Some medicine men were recognised as curers. Either as part of a curing dance, or in a 'special curing' ritual which did not require a full dance, they were said to draw sickness from the bodies of their patients and then to 'sneeze' it out of their noses. This curing procedure often induced a nasal haemorrhage, and the blood was rubbed on the patient in the belief that its smell would keep evil away. Numerous paintings depict such dances. One at Lonyana shows men dancing around a hut in which a recumbent person is being treated by a medicine man. Some of the men are dancing with sticks, as they still do in the Kalahari. A couple of figures have their hands raised in what may be the clapping posture adopted by the women who, on such occasions, clap and sing the medicine songs. Some paintings show the clapping women with individually drawn fingers, so important was their distinctive contribution to the ritual. The arrows lying on the ground in the lower part of the Lonyana painting may depict the mystical 'arrows of sickness' which, it was feared, could bring sickness and even death if the medicine men were not successful.

19

In addition to the healers, the southern San recognised two further categories of medicine men: medicine men of the game and medicine men of the rain. The medicine men of the game were believed to control the movements of antelope herds so that they would run into the waiting hunter's ambush. This 'supernatural' activity assisted the driving of game in which a number of people, both men and women, participated. In the paintings these medicine men are often shown wearing caps with antelope ears attached; the southern Bushmen believed that the game would follow the wearer of such a cap. By this and other techniques the medicine men were sometimes able to thwart the trickster-deity /Kaggen who was believed to be the protector of the large antelope, his especially loved creatures. The name /Kaggen means 'mantis', but the trickster could not be confused with the praying mantis insect; that was only one of his many manifestations. /Kaggen resorted to various ruses to frustrate the hunters, and the medicine men of the game tried to counteract his mischievous influence.

Similarly, the rain-makers were said to outwit and capture a mythical but often dangerous 'rain-animal' so that they could lead it over the parched land where they finally killed it, its blood and

6   J. M. Orpen's 1873 copy of a painting depicting medicine men leading a rain-animal. Two men wear caps with antelope ears and two hold objects which are probably the aromatic herbs used to pacify the 'angry' animal. Colours: red, black and white. Sehonghong, Lesotho.

milk becoming precipitation. Bleek's informants identified a number of rain-animals in the
6 copies of paintings which they were shown. In some paintings the men have attached a rope to the
animal and are leading it across the land.

Especially in the dance, but also in certain other circumstances, the technique employed by the
medicine men to cure, control antelope or make rain was trance performance. Today there is
nothing secret about Bushman trance performance. About half the men and a third of the women
become trancers; they talk freely about their powers and techniques. The /Xam were similarly
open about trance experience, and the Bleek collection contains much on this topic. While the
women clapped and sang the medicine songs, the men danced with increasing vigour. The singing
and the dancing were believed to activate a supernatural potency which made the men tremble,
sweat, experience a rising sensation, bleed from the nose and finally succumb or, as they put it,
'die'. This potency has been likened to electricity because various things can be highly or not so
highly charged with it. In its most intense form it is considered very dangerous, and the modern
!Kung Bushmen say a man could die if he were exposed to it. The medicine men must therefore
learn to control the potency which is said to 'boil' inside them. This potency is important to an
understanding of many paintings, and I refer to it again and again in subsequent chapters.

With proper control of the potency a medicine man can 'die' in trance and yet return from that
frightening experience. In the 'half death' of trance the /Xam medicine men's spirits were
thought to leave their bodies to fight off evil influences, control the game or capture the rain
animal.

7 A painting near Barkly East is one of many showing medicine men entering trance. Some dance
and bend forward with their arms in a backward position or parallel with their bodies. Today some
Kalahari Bushmen still recognise this distinctive posture as that adopted by many medicine men
when they are asking God to put potency into their bodies. The white flecks which surround the
dancers in this painting may represent this potency. After a man has completed his curing rituals
he sits out to recover from trance. In the painting a man covered by a skin cloak is so seated; he is
still bleeding from the nose. The dancers are also wearing the dancing rattles which the southern
Bushmen made from seed pods or from the dried ears of springbok. These were filled with small
stones so that they made a very distinctive swishing sound as the men danced with their short,
pounding steps.

An understanding of the activities of Bushman medicine men is essential to an interpretation of
the art, because some of the medicine men were probably also painters. One early writer was told
of a highly respected man who was both a painter and 'a great rain doctor', and I do not believe he
7 was the only one. Some depictions, indeed, show supernatural entities and events which are said
21, 6, 18 to be seen only by medicine men; these include the potency which the medicine men harness, the
evil which they expel from their bodies and the capture of the 'rain-animal'. The details in such
paintings suggest very strongly that they were painted by those who actually experienced the
hallucinations of trance rather than by others to whom medicine men described their experiences.
This evidence does not, of course, mean that every medicine man was a painter or that every
painter was a medicine man. Some early writers thought that each 'clan' had its own painter or
family of painters. Unfortunately, we have no first-hand accounts of the social position of the
painters, but it seems very unlikely that the position of artists would have been reserved or
hereditary. There is no specialisation in Bushman society, so it is more probable that anyone who

7 A medicine dance in which some dancers bend forward as they enter trance. Blood falls from the noses of those already in trance. The white flecks amongst the dancers probably represent the supernatural potency they are harnessing. Colours: red and white. Halstone, Barkly East.

8   /Gwi men dance in a circular rut around seated women who are clapping the rhythm and singing the medicine songs. The men wear dancing rattles and carry dancing sticks. At a later stage some of the men will enter trance.

23

chose to acquire the skill could have become a painter, as anyone who persevered could become a medicine man. If about half the southern Bushmen were medicine men, as is the case among the modern Kalahari Bushmen, it is very probable that at least some of them would also have been painters.

It is also worth noting that the Bantu-speaking Sotho farmers believed that one of the substances used by the Bushmen in the manufacture of their paint had magical properties which gave protection against hail and lightning. The same substance was also used by Basotho diviners when the bones fell in the position of 'the huts of the Bushmen and Bakalahari [Sotho-speaking Kalahari people]'. Some paintings have been chipped and scratched by Basotho people trying to obtain small quantities of the valued substance. These Sotho beliefs may also point to the association between painting and Bushman medicine men, because many Bantu-speaking people considered the Bushmen to be experts in magical matters such as rain-making.

The identity of the substances used by the Bushmen in making their paints is another point which has given rise to much speculation; its durable qualities are remarkable. A number of early writers commented on the paint and we can obtain from their record some idea of how the paint was made. The red and white pigment seems to have been various coloured earths, haematite and ochres. Black paint might have been made from charcoal or specularite. These materials were ground to a fine powder by means of a small grindstone. The pigment was then mixed with a medium. Numerous writers suggest that this was melted animal fat; ostrich fat was said to be especially effective. Sometimes this mixture was allowed to dry and it was then used as a chalk. The extraordinarily fine lines in some paintings suggest that other paint must have been a free-flowing fluid. In these cases the medium might have been blood or egg-white because tests have determined the presence of amino acids.

The paint was applied by various means. Some early reports mention the use of brushes made by 78 attaching hairs from a wildebeest tail to a small stick. Occasionally brush marks can be detected in thickly applied paint. The use of a thin, hollow bone was also recorded. The bone was filled with paint and used rather like a pen. Some bones might also have been used as spatulas for the application of thicker paint. No doubt artists had their own particular preferences, but whatever they used was sometimes capable of producing amazingly fine lines even on fairly rough surfaces. The artists do not appear to have prepared the uneven rock face in any way prior to painting and depictions often extend over cracks and inequalities in the rock. Some paintings are done in corners so that the front part of an antelope is at right angles to the rest of the body. It has been claimed that artists used hollows or protuberances in the rock face to give three-dimensional shape to parts of their paintings, but this is so rarely found that it could not have been a generally accepted technique. Although some paintings appear to enter or leave cracks, variations in the rock face were ignored rather than exploited.

Even allowing considerable skill in the application of paint with brushes or fine bones, the confidence with which the paintings are drawn is very striking. Mistakes and unfinished paintings are not common; the artists seem to have worked without hesitation. One early report suggests that they first outlined the painting with a burnt stick and then filled it in with paint. Another writer was told that the artists first sketched the depictions in miniature on a small stone before doing the final painting on the wall of the rock shelter.

The fullest account of how the Bushmen painted was recorded by Mary How in 1930. She had managed to contact a very old Phuthi man, Mapote, who, as a child, had painted with Bushmen in their caves; some of his half-brothers had a Bushwoman mother. First Mapote selected a fairly porous piece of rock which would absorb the paint. Then he made a number of brushes by fixing small feathers in the ends of tiny reeds. For black paint he used charcoal mixed with water, and for the white a powdered clay mixed with the thick juice of a plant, *Asclepia gibba*. The red paint was more elaborately prepared. For this Mapote said he required a substance called *Qhang Qhang*, a form of haematite. It had to be prepared at full moon by a woman who heated it until it was red hot; it was then ground between two stones. Finally, Mapote asked for the blood of a freshly killed eland. No eland being available, he had to be content with ox blood; the haematite was the only pigment he mixed with blood. He then said he would paint an eland because 'the Bushmen of that part of the country were of the eland'. He began at the animal's chest and moved his feather brush 'smoothly without the slightest hesitation'. After completing two elands he went on to paint a hartebeest, a lion, two Bushmen and a Mophuti man.

Mary How's account is interesting for a number of reasons. It gives the best and most detailed description we have of an artist at work. But Mapote also supplied a valuable clue to the meaning of the paintings when he said, somewhat cryptically, that the Bushmen were 'of the eland'. In , 92–3, 99, 102 subsequent chapters I refer repeatedly to the eland, the most frequently painted antelope, and try to explain why it is so prominent in Bushman thought and art. For it is not only the paintings which focus attention on the eland; the eland also features in an episodic myth and in a series of important rituals.

Mapote painted his eland in the early years of the twentieth century; today no painters remain. He was the last of a long and astonishing tradition of artists. Just how long that tradition might have been is a controversial problem to which I turn in the following chapter.

CHAPTER THREE

Time and space

Barrow, like every writer since, wondered about the antiquity of the paintings. He was told that some were new; others had been in the shelter since the first white settlers arrived in that part of the country. Today we are still uncertain about the age of much southern African rock art, but recent discoveries have revealed a startling antiquity for at least some examples.

The oldest date so far obtained for rock paintings in southern Africa comes from Eric Wendt's excavation in the Apollo 11 shelter, southern Namibia. He found seven fragments of painted stone in a deposit which was dated by associated charcoal to at least 19 000, and probably as much as 26 000, years before the present. These ancient paintings therefore date from the end of the Middle Stone Age and the very beginning of the Later Stone Age. Unfortunately, only a few stones were found and it is therefore impossible to form a very clear idea of the style and subject matter

42 favoured at this remote period. The stones do, however, show that the artists had mastered the use of two colours and were painting recognisable animals such as rhinoceros. Two of the fragments

43 fit together and bear a painting of an animal of feline proportions but with human hind legs which seem to have been added after the original legs had faded somewhat. It is remarkable that even in this very early period the fusion of animal and human forms was already part of the painters' thought; as subsequent chapters of this book show, such therianthropic paintings were still being executed at the end of the painting tradition. We cannot, of course, be sure if the very early Apollo 11 therianthrope had the same meaning as those later examples; speculation is nonetheless intriguing.

Whatever the meaning of the depictions, the important Apollo 11 discoveries call in question the oft-suggested connection between the European Palaeolithic art and the southern African art. Some writers argue for the diffusion of rock art from Palaeolithic Franco-Cantabria, through north Africa and the Sahara, down the eastern side of the continent to the most recent art of the historical Bushmen, and such dates as were formerly available appeared to confirm this movement. The Apollo 11 stones, however, now show that the most ancient southern African art was contemporary with at least some of the European Palaeolithic art. The two arts therefore probably had independent origins.

In the southern Cape, excavations have associated painted stones with more recent periods. At

45 Boomplaas cave near Oudtshoorn the Deacons found four in strata which could be dated by radiocarbon. The dates range from the beginning of the Christian era to the seventh millennium B.P. Other painted stones from the southern coast have been dated to four and five thousand years

44 before the present. One of the most interesting, the Coldstream stone, was excavated before the development of modern dating techniques, and so its age remains unknown. It was said to have been found placed over the skeleton of a Later Stone Age burial. If this was indeed so, the find provides unusually convincing evidence for the ritual use of at least some Bushman rock art. The paintings on the Coldstream stone depict three human figures with features such as the conventionalised type of head, which are indistinguishable from paintings still on the walls of rock shelters in the neighbouring mountains. A stone from Boomplaas also has a painting very like the Drakensberg art: it is a standing, bichrome eland that could easily be mistaken for one painted by Mapote at the beginning of this century. There is therefore nothing in the subject matter to suggest that the ancient southern mobile art differed significantly from that still preserved on the walls of the rock shelters.

A connection between the southern Cape stones and the far more ancient Apollo 11 stones is impossible to establish. The two periods might have been parts of a continuous tradition, as I suspect, or they may represent two discrete arts; only future discoveries will settle this question.

Most Bushman paintings are, however, not on portable stones but on the walls of rock shelters. The age of these is far more difficult to determine. Edgar Denniger has attempted to use photochromatography to date the amino acids which were part of the binders used in the manufacture of the paint. A horse painted in black at Giant's Castle was dated by this method to

78-9 100 B.P., and this date is confirmed by the historical record which shows that horses were first seen in the Drakensberg at about this period. The other end of the amino acid time scale, which goes back to 800 B.P., may be less reliable. It is difficult to assess the possible contamination of paintings which are so exposed; the longer they have been exposed, the greater the chance that they have been contaminated by, for example, rock-rabbit urine. The dates obtained by this method are considerably younger than those determined by radiocarbon techniques for the buried stones. This may be explained quite simply by a shorter life expectancy for paintings exposed in a rock shelter. On the other hand, there may be a systematic error in the chromatographic method. The decomposition of the amino-acids was calibrated by using whitewashes and other paints of known date in German cathedrals. Although some of the more recent dates obtained for southern African rock paintings, like the Giant's Castle horse, correlate well with dates obtained from historical sources for the same paintings, we cannot be sure that the other end of the time scale in southern Africa will be the same as that in Germany. Furthermore, if the binder used by the Bushmen cannot be positively identified, it is impossible to know how many amino acids were originally present; the number of decayed acids cannot then be computed. The results of this interesting method are therefore suggestive rather than conclusive.

In the absence of reliable absolute dating techniques for paintings on the walls of rock shelters

105 workers have resorted to relative dating based on superpositions. As in many parts of the world, southern African rock paintings are frequently done one on top of another. The upper painting must, of course, be younger than the one on which it is superimposed, but just how much younger is always uncertain. Although superpositions seem to offer a foolproof way of establishing a sequence, the method has serious problems and the proposed sequences differ greatly. Most

writers who have tried to establish a sequence have depended upon the subjective identification of ill-defined 'styles'. The suggested chronology of the 'styles' is sometimes based on superpositions, but it is more often, like the definition of the 'styles' themselves, purely intuitive and makes the unwarranted assumption that the art developed from simple to complex forms. The clear definition of a 'style' is notoriously elusive, but any scheme which is so vague that it cannot be repeated by other workers is of no value. The Abbé Breuil, for instance, working in four shelters in the eastern Orange Free State, believed he could distinguish two main periods comprising a total of no fewer than seventeen phases which unfortunately confuse 'style' with subject matter. Wilhelm Bleek's daughter, Dorothea, after an examination of eighty-eight shelters in the same region, quite understandably found it impossible to concur with the Abbé. More than fifty years ago Miles Burkitt expressed concern over subjectivity such as Breuil's: 'The observer who has carefully looked at the various paintings in several sites will probably find it far easier to recognise the different styles than to explain their differences.' Objectivity in rock art studies is very important, and the unequivocal definition of style remains a challenge to students of Bushman art.

The most reliable sequence so far published avoids this problem. By a quantitative analysis of 1600 superimposed paintings in the southern Drakensberg Patricia Vinnicombe was able to distinguish four phases in a continuous tradition; she wisely does not attempt to define 'styles'.

The first and earliest phase is only fragmentarily preserved. Horizontal blocks of dark red or maroon appear as a stain on the rock rather than a layer of paint adhering to the surface. The shape of these stains suggests the bodies of antelope rather than the vertical human figure. It would, however, be rash to assume that human figures were not painted in this early phase, because the paintings are very poorly preserved. The more fugitive whites and blacks have not lasted, and the paintings are often further obscured by superpositions. The reliably dated painted stones from the southern Cape shelters suggest that the early phases might have been characterised by a wider range of subject matter than these first-phase parietal paintings suggest. It is, however, impossible to connect this early phase with the buried stones: they might have been contemporary, or there might have been a considerable time gap between them.

Vinnicombe's second phase is much better understood. It is now possible to distinguish animals and human figures, some of which are arranged in clear groups. Also distinguishable is a range of colours. Although most paintings are monochromes, both men and antelope are sometimes painted in red and white. The white usually forms the human face and the under-belly of eland or other antelope. Where the more fugitive white paint has faded, only the top of the head and neck remains, or, in the case of the antelope, only the upper red part of the body. Details which may be interpreted as beads or other decorations are often part of the human figures.

92 The third phase contains most of the shaded polychrome paintings which are such a distinctive feature of Bushman art. Adjacent colours, usually red and white, are sensitively blended to give the effect of the antelope's natural colouring and also the shape of its shoulder and belly.

25 Furthermore, some antelope are painted as if seen from the front or from the rear, a remarkable feat of draughtsmanship. Often antelope are painted in surprising detail: they have eyes, mouth, ears, cloven hoofs and occasionally a twisted horn which seems to suggest a specific animal. The human figures are also more finely drawn and frequently show facial markings and ornaments.

7, 65, 94, 100 The large, animated groups of people dancing and performing other activities date principally from this period. Despite these developments, the monochromes and unshaded polychromes of the second phase persist. We should not forget that at least some of the older paintings were visible to the later artists and there is no reason why they should not have continued to paint similar depictions despite the development of new techniques like shading; the new techniques did not completely supplant the older. This persistence of older types of painting does, of course, often make it very difficult to allot a given painting to a specific phase.

Vinnicombe believes that the shaded polychromes diminish in the fourth and final phase. This brief period is most notable for its exotic subjects. White settlers are depicted with their rifles, hats, garments and horses. In the western Cape there is even a painting of a four-masted sailing ship. These new subjects, and also the depiction of Bantu-speaking herders and their cattle, are, in themselves, no reason to suppose a general shift in the Bushman economy. These paintings come from a time when Bushman social structure was under considerable strain, but they were nevertheless done by hunters who clung to their traditional way of life. Colours now include ochre, orange and a bright vermilion, but the paint appears to last less well, so these final paintings are often more poorly preserved than those of earlier phases. Perhaps the artists found it increasingly difficult to find the best materials. If, as I pointed out in the previous chapter, eland blood was an ingredient of the red paint, the near extinction of this antelope by the middle of the nineteenth century might have adversely affected the manufacture of durable paint.

Throughout these four phases there is a continuing numerical emphasis on the eland and an increasing emphasis on the human figure. There is, however, no suggestion that the art may be divided into discrete periods or styles; each phase grades into the next and we can be confident that we are dealing with a single developing tradition. When more sophisticated techniques for absolute dating are developed it may be possible to define the chronology of the four phases more accurately; for the present we must be satisfied with relative dating.

Dating the rock engravings of the interior is even more difficult. They are on exposed rocks and cannot therefore be confidently associated with adjacent stone artefacts or deposits. Nor is there any paint which can be subjected to chemical analysis. Some workers have attempted to construct a sequence of styles or periods based on the degree of patination. This approach has little chance of success because we do not know how deeply the engravings were originally cut into the rock, or how quickly the patina forms. The development of the patina depends upon a number of imponderable factors, such as exposure to sunlight and humidity, which may vary considerably within a site, let alone between sites.

To avoid these difficulties Karl Butzer and his associates have recently attempted to date engravings by climatological and geomorphological methods. The fine, hairline engravings appear to be the oldest, and these were followed by animal representations made in the 'pecking' technique and, finally, geometrics. The so-called classical engravings of animals which show skin folds and other details may be as old as 3200 years, while the geometrics seem to date from about 1300 B.P.

Some of the results of this study have been recently confirmed by Francis Thackeray's remarkable discovery of engraved portable stones in sealed deposits in the Wonderwerk cave near Kimberley. Two of the stones bear fine-line engravings of animals (one is a clear zebra) and others have complex geometric forms. Radiocarbon dates from the strata in which the stones were found range from about 4000 to 10 000 years B.P. The antiquity of the fine-line engravings suggested by

29

9 Rubbing of a rock engraving depicting a recumbent zebra. The engraving has been made by the 'pecking' technique and shows the animal's characteristic strips. The zebra is 35.5 cm long. Doornhoek, western Transvaal.

geomorphological methods is thus confirmed, although it now appears that at least some geometrics are much older than has hitherto been believed. On the other hand, we should remember that work on the comparatively small portable stones might have required different techniques from those suitable for engraving the large, fixed rocks of the open sites.

Nevertheless, this important excavation has shown that engraving, like painting, has a long tradition in southern Africa. Rather than one evolving out of the other, it seems that they developed simultaneously in different environments. Whereas the paintings are found principally in the rock shelters of the mountains which form the edge of the southern African plateau, the

10 A: Engraving of a zebra on a broken piece of portable stone dated to 3990 ± 60 B.P. B: Stone with engraved geometric pattern dated to 5180 ± 70 B.P. Scale in centimetres. Wonderwerk Cave, Kimberley.

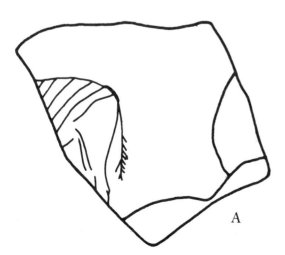

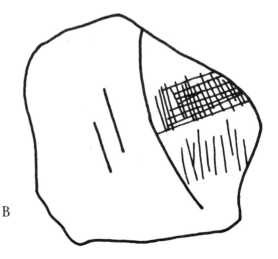

A

30

B

11 Engravings of eland and men. The boulders on which the engravings were done lie exposed in the semi-arid veld. Scale in inches and centimetres. Site: Springbok Oog, Cape Province.

12 Rock engraving of men apparently dancing around eland. Site: Kinderdam, Transvaal.

11 engravings are restricted to the semi-arid plains of the interior where there are hardly any shelters in which to paint. The two art forms have much in common, but there are also differences. Most writers have tended to emphasise the differences at the expense of the similarities and have so consigned the engravings to a quite separate category. It is true, for instance, that the paintings, at

12 any rate the more recent phases, show a higher percentage of human than animal representations, as well as much more complex groupings; human figures and groupings are rare in the engravings.

12, 108 But there are also a number of detailed points of similarity. There is at many of the engraving sites

12 the same marked numerical emphasis on eland to which I have already referred. Other depictions found in both art forms include buck-headed figures, men apparently dancing around eland, creatures with erect hair, eared serpents and human figures with the characteristic 'bar' across the penis. Whatever the differences may be, these shared details seem to indicate that both art forms were the product of a single cognitive system. Their exact relationship, however, remains the subject of research.

The distinction between the engravings and the paintings is the most noticeable feature in the geographical distribution of the southern African rock art. The paintings may be further subdivided into regions, but, as with the temporal phases, the regions are not distinct and discrete. They do not represent exclusively the work of different peoples, although this extreme

13 view has been suggested. The following is an account of the generally accepted geographical grouping of southern African rock art; I give it in only the broadest terms, because much work has still to be done on this important problem.

26–33 The most northerly group, Region I, comprises the art of Zimbabwe and parts of the northern Transvaal. The paintings here are chiefly naturalistic depictions of animals and human beings in monochrome, bichrome and polychrome. In Zimbabwe, trees, grass and fruit are also known; these are very rare elsewhere. As in all other regions, paintings of human beings outnumber paintings of animals. The animals painted include kudu, giraffe, sable antelope, elephant, hippopotamus and buffalo, but the eland which is numerically predominant in some other regions is far less frequently painted. Some paintings at Diana's Vow are well-known because of interpretations published by Frobenius in the 1930s. He believed the recumbent, 'masked' figure to be the body of a king prepared for burial and that the adjacent paintings depicted attendants and sacrificial offerings. Today this regal explanation seems less likely, and the paintings are better understood in terms of the Bushman concepts I outline in Chapters Five and Six. Superimposed on such Bushman paintings there are sometimes thickly painted geometric forms which are probably the work of cattle-herding Bantu-speakers. Geometric forms are more common to the north in Zambia and Malawi where they have been associated with the rituals of the Nyau cult.

There seems to be a strong link between these Zimbabwean paintings and those in Namibia (Region II). The similarities have led some writers to suggest a migration route from east to west between these two areas. In Namibia there is a similar range of colour from simple monochromes to elaborate polychromes which are often painted in considerable detail. Unlike Zimbabwe the Namibian landscape is generally arid, with stark inselbergs rising from the parched plains. One of these mountains is the Brandberg, a veritable treasure-house of art. Although the aspect of the Brandberg is forbidding, the upper valleys and plateaux can be remarkably hospitable after rains; streams often cascade over the entrances to numerous shelters and fill the clear, shallow 'pans'. In a shelter in this rocky fastness is one of the most celebrated of all rock paintings, 'The White Lady of the Brandberg'. This imposing painting was made famous by the romantic treatment it received from the Abbé Breuil. Today few, if any, students of rock art would accept that it depicts a white woman with Mediterranean features, as the Abbé claimed. It seems certain that the profile is not depicted at all and that Breuil was misled by natural markings on the rock; furthermore, the presence of the 'bar' across the penis (very clear in the earliest sketch) and the bow and arrows which the figure carries point clearly to a male Bushman or perhaps a Herero.

Namibia also has numerous engraved sites, the most outstanding of which is Twyfelfontein. People have for centuries, perhaps millennia, been attracted to the perennial spring which flows between the tumbled, scorched rocks on which there are hundreds of engravings of animals, geometric designs, animal spoor, human figures and even footprints. One of the most interesting is a lion which has finely done lion spoor in place of feet and another paw-print at the end of its exaggerated tail. Overlooking the engravings is a rocky terrace with painted shelters and a rich scatter of stone artefacts.

An interesting feature of the Namibian art is the handprints. These are found even more frequently to the south in the shelters of the western Cape, thought by some to be an extension of Region I. All the handprints are positive: paint was applied to the hand which was then placed against the rock face. Negative or stencilled prints, like those of the European Palaeolithic art which were made by applying paint around the hand, are unknown. Nevertheless, the western Cape imprints are of two kinds. One is clearly a fully painted hand, while the other type was stylised by painting lines from the thumb, round the palm, to the little finger, from the first finger to the third and then another curve within that. When a hand so prepared was placed against the rock it left a very distinctive pattern. Both full and stylised handprints are often found in the same shelter. Careful measurements of the imprints have been shown to conform to the hand size of

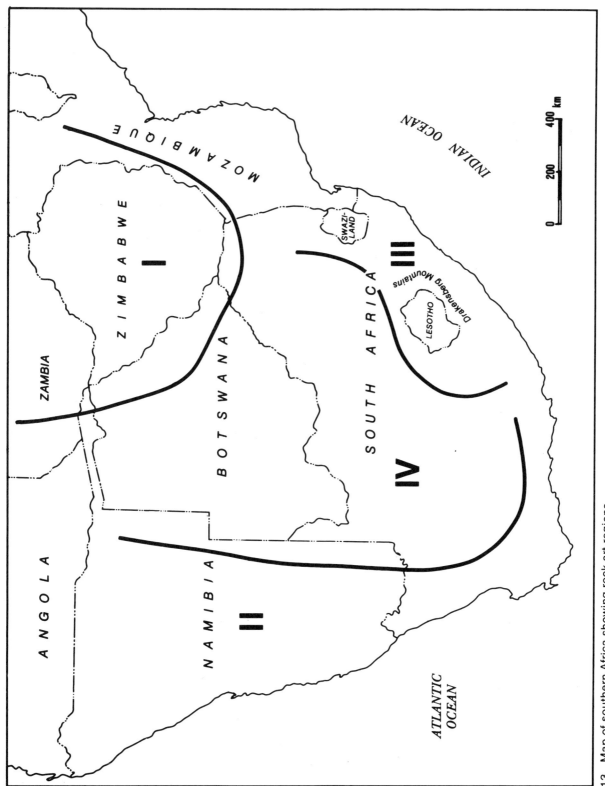

13   Map of southern Africa showing rock art regions.

modern Bushmen, so it seems that the imprints were done by the same people who made the other paintings. On the other hand, the virtual restriction of the imprints to Namibia and the western and southern Cape suggests that they might be the work of the pastoral Khoikhoi (Hottentots) who formerly inhabited these regions.

50 Paintings of the Hottentots' sheep are also fairly numerous. The earliest radiocarbon dates so far obtained for sheep in the southern Cape range from the first to the fourth century A.D. The same people also herded cattle, at any rate in more recent centuries; the absence of paintings of cattle in the region is therefore curious.

Another characteristic feature of the south-western region is the so-called 'hooked head' of many human figures. The back of the neck and top of the head was painted in red, the face being

52, 44 filled in with white paint. Often the fugitive white paint fades to leave a characteristic 'question mark'. Some human figures are painted in fairly elaborate polychrome, but more often they are rather static monochromes.

51 Unlike the art further to the north, the eland is prominent amongst the painted subjects in the

46 south-western Cape. There is also a lesser but still distinct numerical emphasis on elephant; some

47 are surrounded by curious lines which recall the lines occasionally drawn around the rain-animals further to the east.

57–105 The paintings of this western region contrast in certain marked ways with those of the eastern Cape and the south-eastern mountains (Region III). As I have already pointed out, handprints are rarely found to the east. Moreover, the eastern paintings seem much more animated and more finely detailed than those of the west; the very complex groups of human figures which are so characteristic of the east are rare in the west. Nevertheless, despite these differences, the west and east have much in common. The hooked heads, in one form or another, are found in both regions, as are other details like the bar across the penis and men with antelope heads, which, I have already pointed out, are also found to the north in Zimbabwe and in the engravings of the central plateau. Furthermore, the painters of both the west and the east emphasised the eland. In the east, however, it is often painted in shaded polychrome, a technique not found in the west. The

92 paintings of the eastern mountains are in many ways the climax of Bushman art. The delicate

7 shading, the foreshortened antelope in a variety of postures, the animated dances and other

64, 68, 74 groups, and the wealth of curious fantasy depictions which some have called 'mythological' are an endless source of fascination and wonder.

103 The southern part of this region has many paintings of cattle and cattle raids. Patricia Vinnicombe believes it is possible that some of the paintings depict specific raids for which there is historical evidence. Conflict over scarce resources is also reflected in paintings of fights between Bushmen and Bantu-speakers, and even between different Bushman groups. These scenes of conflict seem to date from the final century or so of the Bushmen's life in these parts; the incursions of the white farmers almost exterminated the vast herds of game, while their grazing

83–4 cattle tended to destroy plant resources. One painting shows British soldiers shooting at a herd of

85–7, 89–90 eland and another depicts Boers and their Bantu-speaking servants pursuing Bushman cattle rustlers.

Quite different paintings are found on the central plateau (Region IV). Although some animals are painted here, the paintings are usually thickly drawn monochrome geometric designs such as grids, circles, crosses and dots. These forms are also engraved in great profusion at many sites. At

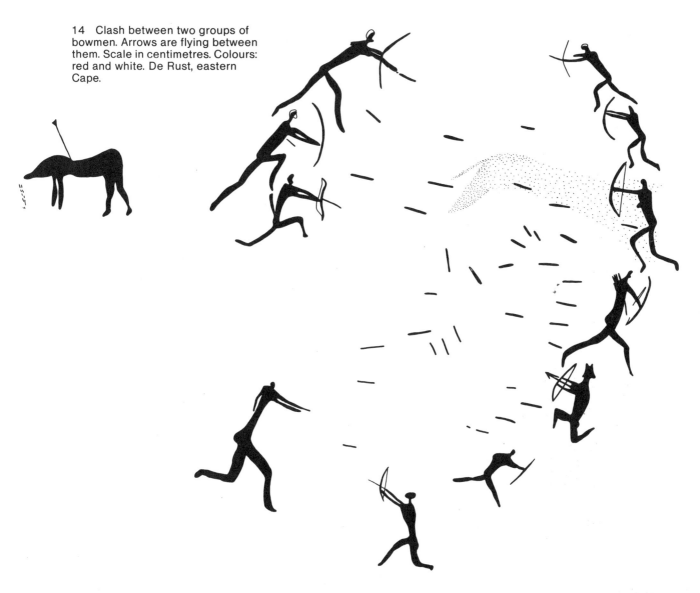

14 Clash between two groups of bowmen. Arrows are flying between them. Scale in centimetres. Colours: red and white. De Rust, eastern Cape.

Driekopseiland, near Kimberley, there are approximately three thousand engravings. It is, indeed, the engravings which are the principal feature of the interior plateau. The geometric designs, whether painted or engraved, have attracted much speculation. Even Barrow wondered if they were 'intended to express some meaning'. Recently a writer has suggested that some engravings at Driekopseiland are characters from an ancient Libyan script and convey a rather feeble message. Such interpretations are, however, only possible by selecting a few designs from the many thousands which cover the striated rock surface. So this and other bizarre interpretations, which include the identification of Phoenician boats and Egyptian symbols, should be rejected. At present we have no idea what most of these prolific designs mean. Nevertheless, other engravings in various regions do seem to represent the settlement patterns of Iron Age, Bantu-speaking farmers. These should not be confused with the apparently older and enigmatic 'abstract' designs.

I have not dwelt at any length on the regional distribution of the southern African rock art, because it is little understood. Many writers publish maps showing regions, but it is not always clear what the regions mean. Do they delimit groups of people defined by race, economy, language; or a single racial, economic and linguistic group which happened to produce slightly different types of art because of the comparative isolation of groups? It is true that anyone familiar with the art can often assign a given example to, say, either the western Cape or the south-eastern mountains. But this is purely intuitive, and the meaning of such differences as may be discerned is obscure.

The geographical divisions therefore usually amount to little more than lines on maps; the exact criteria used to define the items enclosed by the lines are left vague. To avoid such subjectivity, the classification of rock art, as with the classification of any other data, must have a specific and explicitly stated purpose. This purpose will govern selection of discriminating features for the creation of classes. Writers on southern African rock art have erred in assuming that a single inherent order in the paintings awaits discovery. This is misleading. There are, in fact, multiple orders depending upon the choice of discriminating features. For instance, the fundamental dichotomy between paintings and engravings first made in the last century by George Stow and then by all other writers since is based on a single, arbitrarily selected feature – technique. If, on the other hand, a different criterion were selected (say, a defined proportion of eland to other species), a quite different regional classification of the rock art would result; it would cross-cut the now widely accepted regions which I have described, but it would be equally valid.

The solutions to the problems of southern African rock art distribution lie in the future. For the present, we can note that there do not appear to be any radical regional differences. Even the much discussed distribution of paintings and engravings may not be very significant. All regions share a great many features, no matter what their differences might be. By and large, it seems fair to conclude that the general uniformity of the art supports the conclusion I drew from the ethnography: the Bushmen over most of southern African shared a single cognitive system which had regional variations.

Furthermore, virtually all the art, whether paintings or engravings, whether in Zimbabwe or in the southern Cape, is clearly associated with a hunter–gatherer economy and may be confidently ascribed to the Bushmen. If other people did learn to paint, perhaps from the Bushmen themselves, they made only a very minor contribution to the art as a whole. There are, in fact, references to some Bantu-speaking agriculturalists (like Mapote) trying their hand at painting, but rock art was never a feature of the southern Bantu culture. It has also been argued that the sheep- and cattle-herding Hottentots might have been responsible for some of the paintings, such as those of sheep, in the south-western Cape. Whilst it is no doubt possible that some Hottentots attempted painting, like those Bantu-speakers, the art is essentially hunter–gatherer in content and probably in authorship as well.

The general uniformity of the art in both space and time holds important implications for interpretation. There is a clear continuity through time from the modern ethnography on the Kalahari Bushmen to the ethnography collected from the nineteenth-century Bushmen and thence to the unbroken painted record which stretches back into antiquity. We can, therefore, with due circumspection, use the ethnography to interpret at least the more recent phases of the art. This is, however, easier said than done. Writers on rock art have long had access to the ethnography, yet they have made surprisingly little use of it. The reason for their neglect is twofold. First, in dealing with the art itself they have depended too heavily on personal impressions and selectivity; there has been a tendency to concentrate on immediately attractive paintings, especially the apparently explicit 'scenes of Stone Age life'. Secondly, they have not known how to handle the ethnography. Very little of it is directly related to the art; one cannot get at the ideas expressed in the art unless one can distil from the ethnography the vital concepts and then show how they are transformed into graphic representations. Failing to appreciate these two points, some writers have tried to match specific paintings with incidents in specific myths; the results are singularly unconvincing. Because both art and belief was shared by the whole Bushman community, we must look, not at selected and possibly idiosyncratic examples of either, but at generalised and repeated features. In the following two chapters I therefore show first how the art can be studied with minimum subjectivity, and then how certain repeated features of the art express beliefs preserved in the ethnography.

CHAPTER FOUR

Facts and theories

The problems which we encountered in the last chapter clearly point to the need for objective and quantitative techniques. In the past most writers were content to select only the best preserved or what they deemed the most interesting or most beautiful paintings for study. Rock art enthusiasts are insatiable and constantly seeking 'better' paintings, often in more and more remote places.

Some writers had particular interests which they pursued or themes which they followed up. This eclectic trend started over a hundred years ago when George Stow, one of the great pioneers of rock art studies in southern Africa, collected copies of paintings 'to compile a history of the manners and customs of the Bushmen, as depicted by themselves'. Archaeologists ever since have assumed the art to be a pictorial record of Stone Age life which they can use to supplement their excavations. The art does indeed illustrate some 'prehistoric' customs, but in southern Africa these are usually known first from historical or ethnographic sources and only then identified in the art. Very little about the material or social life of the Bushmen has been gleaned exclusively from the art.

In selecting paintings to illustrate a particular custom, such as dancing or hunting, or to exemplify supposed styles and painting techniques, writers are often selective in a more restricted sense: they take one or two depictions from a panel of, perhaps, a hundred individual paintings. The overall coherence of these complex panels is an important point to which I return in Chapter Six.

It has, then, become increasingly clear that an interpretation of the art must not depend upon grossly selective and consequently inaccurate work. In this chapter I describe some of the techniques that have been developed to introduce more objectivity into the study of southern African rock art. There can be little doubt that these methods transformed the subject and opened up the way to new and more convincing interpretations. I therefore show how the results of quantification make the traditionally accepted explanations of hunting magic and 'art for art's sake' no longer tenable and also point to the quite different approach I outline in Chapters Five and Six.

The need for objective and comprehensive research was first emphasised in the 1960s by Tim Maggs and Patricia Vinnicombe; since then a number of quantitative projects have been published. Each of these studies is confined to a clearly defined geographical area. *All* the paintings in the area are recorded, or, if this is not practicable because of the vast number of paintings, a valid sample. The first stage in the recording process is, of course, the location of sites; once discovered, they can be plotted on large-scale maps. In rugged terrain this is an arduous task; every shelter, no matter how small, must be inspected. Results of such intensive searches so far 58, 26 published show that most painted sites are rock shelters, but paintings also occur on large boulders which are sometimes surprisingly exposed to the weather.

Unlike many of the European Palaeolithic caverns, most of the southern African sites could have been living-places. Although it is generally impossible to relate paintings to the deposits in a shelter, it is worth noting that at Barkly East, three-quarters of the painted sites contain surface scatters of stone artefacts referable to a Later Stone Age industry. There is also a tendency for the aspect of sites to range between east and north-west; at Barkly East 89% of the sites face between 98 these two compass directions and so enjoy maximum sunshine. The generally colder and damper south-facing shelters were avoided. Most painted shelters make very comfortable living-places.

58, 69 Some large shelters with many paintings are surrounded by a number of smaller sites with fewer paintings. These groups of sites might have been the places where a number of camps congregated after the start of the summer rains, as I described in Chapter Two. An early writer claimed that these caves were the 'rallying-points for the various clans'. Although 'clans' is an inappropriate term, the observation suggests that these large shelters were indeed the places where camps amalgamated and were thus the equivalent of waterholes in the drier regions where there are far fewer rock shelters. Other, more isolated, sites with few paintings might have been temporary bivouacs used by hunters out on overnight expeditions.

Occasionally one finds a painted site which could not have been a living-site. One of these was a 92 small, overhanging rock with a magnificent panel of eland in various postures painted on its underside. The rock on which this masterpiece was painted has now been removed to the Natal Museum, Pietermaritzburg, for safe keeping. Sites like this are difficult to interpret; perhaps the people lived nearby in huts which have now disappeared. It would be wrong to assume that these comparatively rare sites in themselves suggest esoteric motives, as do the deep caverns of western Europe.

Once all the sites in the study area have been located, the time-consuming recording of the paintings can begin. All workers who have undertaken quantitative studies have in some way followed a system of recording originally proposed by Pat Vinnicombe. The system aims at noting a large number of features of each individual painting so that significant correlations between variables can be discovered. The danger does, of course, exist that the system will create its own correlations and that these will not be important. The most useful application of any form of numerical analysis is therefore to testing specific hypotheses. No purpose is served by gathering supposedly random data and then analysing them in the hope that something will turn up.

One of the principal advantages of numerical data is that they can be prepared for computer or punch-card analysis. It is doubtful whether it is worth preparing samples of under two thousand paintings for computer analysis, but for larger samples and for the eventual comparison of different geographical areas the computer will prove indispensable. Some of the real differences between areas, at present only intuitively felt, can be expressed in numerical analyses. Preliminary comparisons have, for instance, confirmed the impression that the artists in different regions emphasised different animals; in Namibia, for instance, giraffe and springbok were the most frequently painted animals, while in Zimbabwe kudu and elephant are numerically prominent.

Detailed comparisons between regional studies have, however, been made difficult by the varying criteria and categories used by different workers; so far it has proved impossible to reach unanimity on this fundamental issue. Nevertheless, it has been possible to obtain a good idea of the art of the south-eastern mountains. Four quantitative studies from this richly painted region have been published, and a fifth, large-scale recording project is being undertaken in Lesotho. I shall therefore confine the following remarks to the art of this better known region.

All the samples so far available show a clear but not overwhelming emphasis on human figures and social activities. At Barkly East, for instance, 53.9% of the 2361 recorded paintings are of human beings; most are depicted in social groups. The next largest category comprises antelope. Other animals do not feature prominently in the art, but are nevertheless of great interest. They include felines, elephant, snakes, bushpigs, birds, fish and domestic animals like dogs and cattle. In the Barkly East sample of 1023 paintings of animals there are only 76 such depictions. The emphasis of the art is therefore clearly on antelope.

Further emphases within the antelope category are important for the interpretation of the art. Of the 942 antelope recorded at Barkly East, 62.2% are eland; the next most frequently painted antelope is rhebok, 25.4%. The artists' interest in eland is also shown by the care they took in painting them. More eland (42.2%) are painted in polychrome than rhebok (15.0%). Just as striking as the emphasis on eland is the omission of certain other species, such as wildebeest, which the artists could have painted had they wished.

Results like these make it highly unlikely that Barrow did in fact see paintings of all the animals he lists; certainly, they were not present in the equal proportions he seems to imply. Perhaps he was combining impressions from a number of sites and thus, like many other observers, missing the highly significant repetitive features of the art. Any interpretation of the art must explain the very marked preferences and avoidances confirmed by quantification. I offer such an explanation in Chapter Five.

Another pattern of a different kind revealed by quantification suggests even more strongly that the art is systematic rather than random and that the painters followed certain rules. This system appears in the way artists superimposed one painting upon another. Sometimes paintings are so densely superimposed that, to anyone unfamiliar with the art, the overall effect seems entirely random. The commonly held view is therefore that superpositioning is meaningless. Some writers argue that the artists painted on top of older paintings either because there was no suitable rock left on which they could paint, or because the act of painting was more important than the finished product. Studies at Giant's Castle, Barkly East and elsewhere have suggested, contrary to this view, that superpositioning was not random or accidental, but a deliberate way of linking paintings according to certain conventions.

In the first place, it seems unlikely that the artists painted on top of the work of their predecessors because there was nowhere else to paint. It is true that in some sites all available rock surface has been used, but paintings are also superimposed even where there is a clean surface immediately next to the first painting. This conclusion was borne out by determining the percentage of paintings involved in superpositioning in a number of sites. In one site, for instance,

40

12% of the 232 paintings were in superpositioning; in another, four out of only eight paintings (i.e. 50%) were superimposed. In neither site is the available rock surface suitable for painting exhausted.

So it seems as if the Bushman artists deliberately painted one representation on top of another. This inference is supported by an analysis of the kinds of painting involved in superpositioning: the artists tended to use certain depictions in this way and not others. For instance, at Barkly East, 20.6% of the 586 eland appear in superpositions as upper or lower painting; but only 5.0% of the 240 rhebok and 4.6% of the 1253 human figures were used. The eland was again singled out for special treatment. Furthermore, there was a distinct tendency to paint animals on animals or animals on human figures, but an avoidance of painting human figures on animals. For reasons which are still not entirely clear, the artists preferred certain combinations and avoided others. They were, in fact, arranging the paintings according to rules, even though the total effect of a densely painted panel is apparently confused. Even more interesting, the rules which the painters observed operated over an extensive area. The results I have now cited come from Barkly East; 200 km to the east very similar results have been obtained for superpositions at Giant's Castle and in the Ndedema Gorge.

Quantitative studies are thus able to bring out clearly and unequivocally some of the artists' preferences. First, it can be shown that they selected only certain types of animal from their environment and ignored others which equally were animals that they ate and which they could have painted if they so desired. Then they bestowed the more time-consuming and meticulous treatment of shaded polychrome painting on the eland rather than on other antelope. And, lastly, they arranged the paintings according to certain rules. Because all these conventions are the same over extensive areas we must conclude that the artists were responding to a widely-held cognitive system, rather than to individual whims: the art reflects shared beliefs and values. This uniformity may be explained by the far-flung ties between camps which I described in Chapter Two. The frequent visiting and fluidity of Bushman camp populations clearly assisted the speedy dissemination of new ideas or new painting techniques.

The uniformity of the art over distances of a few hundred kilometres which quantitative studies have confirmed is important in assessing the meaning of the art. With some of the quantified data before us, we can now consider the popular explanations for Bushman rock art which have been widely held and advocated for many years.

Many writers have assumed that the paintings are the product of the artistic impulse of individual painters. It is argued that the Bushman artists were moved by an innate desire to produce beautiful objects; an aesthetic imperative drove them 'to express themselves in paint'. In this view the Bushman rock art is no more than an outstanding efflorescence of primitive aesthetics and is detached from any aspect of social life.

The beauty of so many Bushman rock paintings makes this popular view superficially plausible, but it has severe limitations. In the first place, the aesthetic interpretation concerns the mental states of individual artists. Yet all the evidence of the quantitative studies shows that individual responses played a very minor role in the production of the art. If the individual artist could paint whatever he wished, it is surprising that there is not more variety in the subject matter.

This objection is damaging enough to the aesthetic explanation, but there is also a serious theoretical objection. The mental process or state of mind said to account for the art is inferred

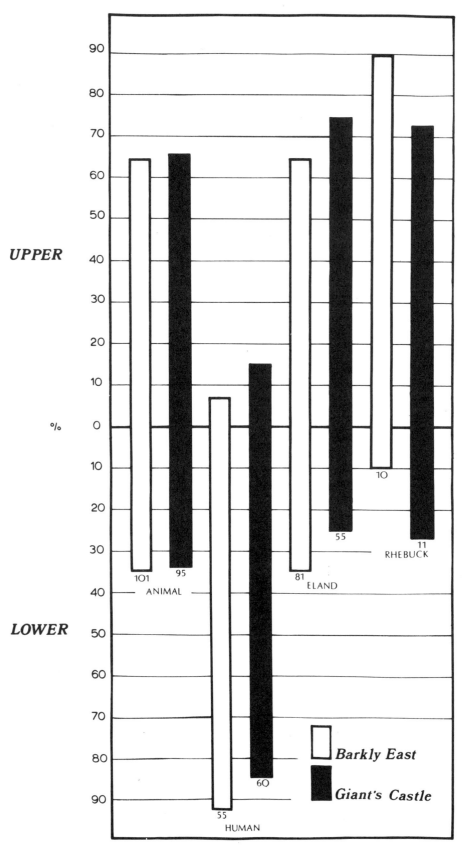

15 Diagram to show proportions of animal and human representations in the upper and lower layers of superpositions at Barkly East and Giant's Castle. There is a distinct tendency in both areas for animals to form the upper elements and human figures the lower.

from the art and then used to explain it; no further evidence for the supposed artistic impulse is ever offered by writers of this persuasion, nor do they test their hypothesis against either the painted or the ethnographic data. The paintings delight the writer, and he therefore assumes that they were done merely to delight the artists and the original viewers. The argument that painting was the result of an innate artistic desire to produce beautiful objects is therefore circular. I do not deny that the artists took great care with their work and that their skill was admired by their contemporaries; the delicacy and fine draughtsmanship of many paintings count against so extreme a position. But these excellencies, amply illustrated in this book, should not be allowed to divert attention from social and religious issues.

Other writers, perhaps influenced by the traditional explanation for the European Palaeolithic paintings, have suggested that the art was associated with sympathetic magic designed to ensure success in hunting. Having noted the large number of painted antelope, writers who hold this view postulate the hunters' anxiety about the outcome of the hunt. To assuage this supposed anxiety, the hunter is said to have devised a type of magic which involved the depiction of animals in the belief that these depictions would guarantee success in the chase. Again, as with the aesthetic explanation, the quantitative studies do not support this suggestion. Hunting is depicted far less frequently than is commonly supposed; Harald Pager found only 29 hunts among the 3909 paintings in the Ndedema Gorge, and in all areas human figures outnumber paintings of animals. The magical explanation is not supported by the facts of the art.

This position is more easily maintained in Europe where nothing is known about the beliefs of the artists, but in southern Africa there is a good deal recorded about Bushman beliefs. In neither the modern nor the nineteenth-century record is there any indication that the Bushmen believed (or still believe) that the manufacture of a representation would have any magical effect. It is certainly true that they believed it possible to influence game and even the weather, but sympathetic magic played no part in these beliefs and rites. Like the art itself, the ethnography does not support the suggestion that a belief in sympathetic magic motivated the Bushman artists.

Even this brief account has made it clear that detailed quantitative studies are a necessary preliminary to the formulation of any theory about the meaning of the art. Quantification of the art has shown that neither of the two most widely proposed explanations can stand up to close scrutiny. At this point the enquiry could easily end in an impasse. The quantitative studies show that the art was a communication system and even disclose the 'grammar' of that system; but quantification elucidates neither the meaning of the elements nor the significance of the ways in which they are combined. To move from structure to meaning we must examine the Bushman ethnography.

But even with the ethnography to guide us, our task is daunting. Only a few nineteenth-century Bushmen were invited to comment directly on specific paintings. Their remarks are, as I show in the next chapter, very valuable indeed, but we still need to discover the more general concepts which the artists expressed in a variety of ways. To do that, and so reach our goal of understanding the art, we must identify the key metaphors which feature in Bushman myth, ritual and, I argue, also in their art.

43

CHAPTER FIVE

Crystallised metaphors

In the preceding chapters I have repeatedly referred to paintings of eland. Indeed, the prominence of this antelope in the art suggests there can be little doubt that it enjoyed some sort of special status in Bushman thought. I therefore now try to answer one of the most important questions that can be asked about southern African rock art: What did all these depictions of eland mean to the artists and their contemporaries?

It could be argued that the eland is the largest and fattest of all antelope and that its desirability as food is sufficient to explain why the Bushmen were so interested in it. It is a most impressive animal in sheer size and stature; a full-grown eland can weigh up to 1200 lbs (545 kg). The eland's great bulk is partially responsible for its being the most easily taken antelope; a hunter can run down an eland, especially in summer, because it soon becomes winded and stands stock-still, sweating and foaming at the mouth. If there is no strong wind, an eland can be separated from the herd and driven back to the hunter's camp before being killed; but, if there is a wind, the eland obstinately runs up-wind even if this means passing close by the hunter. From the Bushmen's point of view this is a very fortunate behavioural characteristic because eland meat is greatly valued, and an eland can provide food for a large number of people for several days. The Bushmen say the heart of an old bull eland is encased in so much fat that a man cannot put his arms around it; melted down, the fat requires the entire eland skin for a suitable container. The Bushmen themselves are very impressed by all these distinctive qualities and talk a great deal about them. One Kalahari Bushman told me, 'All other animals are like servants to the eland'. On the face of it, there seems to be enough quite simple and obvious evidence to explain why the Bushmen painted so many eland.

This straightforward explanation would be convincing were it not for the ethnography. When we turn to the recorded beliefs of the nineteenth-century Bushmen, we find that the eland was important in more ways than simply food. The eland featured in myths and rites which clearly show that it was an important symbol in Bushman thought. I believe that it is the symbolic function, rather than its food value, that explains the prominence of the eland in the art.

To support this suggestion, I turn first to a complex eland myth which was recorded in a number of versions from different informants. A comparison of these versions shows that the full myth is made up of a series of episodes which the narrators could use or omit as they pleased. Some informants dwelt at length on the creation of the eland. In this episode the Mantis, a demi-god or trickster-deity, took a portion of a shoe and placed it in the waterhole. There it grew into a large bull eland. Every day the Mantis fed the eland honey. He loved it greatly and sang for joy about his eland.

Other informants were more interested in the death of the eland than its creation. The following is a version of the eland's death of which only a few lines have hitherto been published. It was dictated in 1873 by one of Bleek's /Xam Bushmen. Because the full verbatim transcription is lengthy, I give a summary, but I retain certain key phrases.

> The people wondered why the Mantis was not bringing home honey, so one day they sent his grandson, the young Ichneumon (a mongoose), with him to find out what he was doing with it. When these two reached the waterhole, the Mantis put the Ichneumon in a skin bag so that he could not see what was happening. The next day the Ichneumon again went with the Mantis, but this time he cut a small hole in the bag. Thus he managed to see the eland come out of the waterhole to eat the honey which the Mantis had placed on a flat stone. When the eland had eaten the honey, it went back into the middle of the reeds. After they had returned to the camp, the Ichneumon went to his cousins, the meerkats, and told them that the Mantis was giving the honey to the eland instead of bringing it home.
>
> The next day, while the Mantis was collecting honey, the Ichneumon took the meerkats to the waterhole. There they imitated the call of the Mantis, and the eland came out of the reeds. When the unsuspecting eland walked up to the flat stone for its honey, one of the meerkats shot it with an arrow. The eland ran away, staggering, and fell dead. Then the Ichneumon and his cousins went to the eland and began to cut it up.
>
> When the Mantis reached his honey, he found it was dry. It seemed as if the eland's blood was coming from the honey. At once he suspected that the young Ichneumon had taken his cousins to the eland and that they had killed it.
>
> He ran to the waterhole, but the eland did not answer his call; he saw the eland's blood on the stone. He wept. Then he followed the eland's tracks to where the Ichneumon and the meerkats were cutting up the eland. He saw that his premonition had been correct. He drew an arrow from his quiver, for he intended to fight the eland's fight. He shot the arrow, but it came back at him and he had to dodge it. The meerkats continued eating the eland's meat which they were cooking, because they knew they were safe. The Mantis shot another arrow, but it too was deflected back at him. So he ran up to the people to strike them with his knobkerrie. He accused them of killing his eland. But one of the meerkats snatched the knobkerrie from the Mantis and beat him with it and then threw the Mantis onto the eland's horns.
>
> The Mantis fled. From a safe distance he commanded his quiver and his shoes to follow him, and they obeyed him. At home he told his wife that the meerkats had beaten him.

There is so much of great interest in this myth that a full exposition would be far too long for this book; I therefore comment on only a few points relevant to understanding the art. The

45

intimate association between the eland and the honey is one such point. The southern Bushmen believed that the eland smelt strongly of honey. Although they do not mention honey specifically, some early writers noted the distinctive aroma of the eland; they commented on the 'strong, sweet perfume' which arises as an eland is skinned, and the 'sweet aromatic smell' this antelope leaves in the grass where it has been lying. The eland's strong scent is important because in Bushman thought scent was one medium for the transference of the supernatural power to which I referred in Chapter Two. The eland and honey were believed to have the same scent and so similar power. This relationship is expressed in numerous paintings in the Drakensberg which depict bees associated with eland. One painting at least makes a further important association by explicitly showing bees swarming above a line of dancing men. In the Kalahari the Bushmen still like to dance when the bees are swarming because they believe they are able to harness their great power. A relationship between bees, honey and dancing was in fact mentioned by one of Bleek's informants who said that the people used a bullroarer to cause the bees to swarm and make honey which they collected in leather bags and took home to the women. When they had satisfied their hunger, the whole camp danced all night, the women clapping and the men pounding their feet until all were enveloped in a cloud of dust. There is, then, a close connection between bees, honey, scent, the eland and the supernatural power which medicine men activate in the trance dance. I must emphasise that these observations in no way exhaust the complex associations of honey in Bushman thought, but they do help to explain a further significant point in this narrative.

When the Mantis discovered that the meerkats had killed his beloved eland, he resolved to 'fight the eland's fight'. In the Bleek translation, this seems to mean that the Mantis was fighting *on*

16   Medicine men wearing dancing rattles and carrying sticks dance along a red line of supernatural potency. The power which they are harnessing is symbolised by the swarm of bees; the roughly rectangular shape is probably a hive. Higher up, three women are also linked by the line of potency; two clap the medicine songs while the third dances. Scale in centimetres. Colours: red and white. Cullen's Wood, Barkly East.

behalf of the eland. This is no doubt correct in the general context of the myth, but it is doubtful whether the Bushman word translated 'fight' can, as a verb, mean anything other than 'fight *against*'; 'to fight the eland's battle' is a peculiarly English idiom. As it stands, the translation therefore obscures the correct meaning which involves a *metaphorical* use of the Bushman word for 'fight'. The word which the narrator used to mean 'fight' was, in some instances, translated 'curse', the closest the Bleeks could come to expressing in English a very dangerous quantity of supernatural potency. Despite major linguistic differences between the two languages the identical Bushman word is still used by the modern !Kung Bushmen to mean 'fight' *and* an exceptional degree of supernatural potency. This modern use of the word tends to confirm my belief that the sentence in question should be construed: 'The Mantis intended to fight against the eland's potency.' When the meerkats killed and skinned the eland, its aromatic odour rose up filled with its potency, and they were able to harness this power to deflect the Mantis's arrows. Evil or sickness was, and in the Kalahari still is, sometimes conceived of as small, invisible arrows which a hostile medicine man could shoot into unsuspecting people. It is evidently against such a supernatural attack that the meerkats were defending themselves by appropriating the eland's extreme potency or 'fight'. The way in which they were able to achieve this feat needs further explanation.

In the Kalahari today Bushman hunters like to 'dance eland potency' next to the carcass of a freshly killed eland. The situation is redolent with the animal's scent and power, and they believe they can exploit this power in their trance performance. The hunters see how much fat – another aromatic substance – is on the eland; then they 'dance in praise of the fat'. A medicine man who has special control of eland potency enters trance and cures all present of known and unknown ills by removing any 'arrows of sickness' which might have been directed against them. In this rather exceptional circumstance the dance is performed by the hunters alone; no women are present. This still happens in parts of the Kalahari. In the south, a hundred and more years ago, the potency of a dead eland was also ritually acknowledged: the man who had shot the eland did not approach the carcass until the heart had been cut out, because it was thought to be imbued with a dangerous degree of potency. Unfortunately, the ethnography does not mention a medicine dance performed next to the carcass, but many paintings show dead eland associated with medicine men and so suggest that the southern people also liked to dance at an eland kill. A successful eland hunt was therefore a significant event for more reasons than the provision of much meat and fat. These extra, ritual associations are important to a proper appreciation of many rock paintings; to understand them we must examine the death of an eland more closely.

The behaviour of a dying eland is, in fact, very striking. One writer has described it thus: 'With deeply-sunk, hollow eyes, the dying creature watches the approach of its enemies. Its body trembles; the fever from the wound causes it to stumble; the nostrils are wide open, owing to the difficulty in breathing; the hair stands on end.' The dying animal also sweats profusely and when it finally succumbs 'melted fat, as it were, together with blood, gushes from its nostrils'. Some of these features were accurately depicted by the Bushman artists. A painting at Martinsdale, for instance, shows an eland which has been separated from the herd by men carrying spears; blood falls from wounds on its flank. The men are accompanied by dogs, one of which leaps at the eland's throat as hunting dogs do. The eland is clearly staggering, and its head is lowered. Some of its hair is standing on end, and blood gushes from its nose. This painting is particularly explicit, but many

17   A wounded and dying eland staggers as it is pursued by spear-carrying men and dogs. It bleeds from the nose and from wounds on its flanks. One spear has broken in striking its hindquarters. The light grey colour of the eland suggests advanced age. Colours: red, light grey and black. Martinsdale, Barkly East.

other somewhat less obvious paintings and engravings also depict dying eland. Some simply have the antelope with its head lowered in a posture that can be mistaken for grazing, and some show only the blood or white foam falling from its nose. The dying eland is, indeed, a frequently painted element in the art, although this has not been generally recognised by western viewers who are unfamiliar with the behaviour of antelope.

The description I have given will already have suggested that the dying eland's behaviour is remarkably like the behaviour of medicine men entering trance, as I described it in Chapter Two. As the intensity of the dance increases, the men sweat profusely and start to tremble violently; their eyes are fixed and they breathe swiftly and shallowly. Trance takes hold of them, and they stagger and finally collapse. At this moment the southern Bushmen frequently bled from the nose, although this happens less frequently in the modern Kalahari. The southern people also believed that hair came out on the back of a man in trance; to prevent this they rubbed him with antelope fat.

There can be little doubt that the death of an eland is comparable with the 'death' of a man in trance, but did the Bushmen themselves recognise the analogous relationship between these two sets of behaviour? In other words, was the death of the powerful eland seen as a metaphor of the 'death' of a medicine man? The answer to this question lies in the art and especially in a very important painting at the Game Pass shelter in the Natal Drakensberg.

The large eland in this painting staggers as its forelegs give way; its head is lowered and the face, turned towards the viewer, clearly shows the 'deeply-sunk, hollow eyes'. The artist thought the erect hair an important feature, so he exaggerated the hair on various parts of the eland's body. This is undoubtedly a dying eland; but the chief interest of this painting lies more in the associated depictions.

In the centre of the group a man dances in the typical posture (bending forward, with arms extended) which the Kalahari Bushmen call 'flying' to describe the experience of trance; a short skin cloak hangs down in front of him. Close inspection reveals that this dancer does not have human feet: one leg at least shows an antelope's hock. Antelope features are still more clearly seen in the figure which holds the eland's tail. This man has distinctly depicted cloven antelope hoofs, and his legs are crossed in imitation of the eland's dying stumble. He also seems to have an antelope head with a clear antelope ear. The antelope head is even more distinct on the figure at the extreme right which also has hoofs and a tail. Interestingly, this figure is covered with erect hair just like that on the eland. The white dots which appear to fall from this man probably represent the sweat of a dancer 'dying' in trance. Just to the left of this complex man–antelope is another figure with antelope head and hocks. Like the meerkats in the myth about the death of the Mantis's eland, these trance dancers are appropriating the potency released by the death of the eland, but, in doing so, they have come to share some of the qualities of the powerful but (paradoxically) dying antelope. So fully do they participate in the potency of the dying eland that they have come to look like the antelope.

This interpretation of the painting is confirmed by a statement obtained by J. M. Orpen from a Bushman in 1873, the same year as Bleek recorded the eland myth. Orpen's informant, Qing, came from the south-eastern mountains and actually took him to some of the painted shelters. When Orpen asked what the paintings of men with antelope heads meant, he replied that 'they were men who had died and now lived in rivers, and were spoilt at the same time as the elands and by the dances of which you have seen paintings'. This is one of the few, and therefore very valuable, comments made by nineteenth-century Bushmen directly on the paintings. The complexity of the statement suggests that, as published, it combines the informant's answers to persistent questioning on a topic which Orpen did not fully understand; indeed, Orpen admits to having made his 'fragmentary' material 'consecutive'.

Not knowing anything about trance performance, Orpen understandably enough took 'died' as a literal explanation rather than in its metaphorical meaning. The informant then went on, probably in response to further questioning, to say that the antelope-headed figures had been 'spoilt . . . by the dances'. He employed this same puzzling phrase to describe medicine men of the rain in a painting depicting the leading of the rain animal, adding that they were spoilt 'because their noses bleed'. Like the metaphorical 'die', 'spoil' is also used by modern Kalahari Bushmen to mean 'to enter deep trance', so it seems that the 'spoil' in Qing's statement is a second trance metaphor. His further explanation that these people 'now lived in rivers' is yet another phrase that can be similarly explained. Being under water was recognised as analogous to the experience of trance: the struggle, gasping for breath, sounds in the ears, a sense of weightlessness, inhibited movement, distorted vision and final loss of consciousness are common to both experiences. A number of southern Bushman accounts of medicine men in trance refer in one way or another to their being under water, and some paintings depict medicine men associated with fish.

The Bushman's explanation of the antelope-headed figures is thus really a series of synonymous metaphors which Orpen, supposing them all to be literal and different in meaning, made consecutive. The informant was actually saying that the paintings of men with antelope heads depicted medicine men who had 'died' or been 'spoilt' in trance and were experiencing something like being under water. His additional statement that these men had been 'spoilt at the same time as the elands and by the dances' probably means that, when the medicine men were in trance, they

18 Medicine men bleeding from the nose in trance attempt to control a rain-animal. Some erect white hairs on the animal suggest that it is near to death. The two fish refer to the similarity between trance experience and being under water. Colours: black, red and white. De Rust, eastern Cape.

were able to harness the potency of dying eland. The men and the eland were simultaneously 'spoilt', the one metaphorically in trance, the other literally in physical death.

59–60   This informant's comments on the antelope-headed figures provide the final and persuasive evidence that the painting at Game Pass shelter brings together, in a very remarkable way, the two elements of what must have been a key metaphor in the thought of the Bushman painters. On the one hand, there is the dying eland, and, on the other, the 'dying' or 'spoilt' medicine men. In many paintings the artists made the analogous relationship even clearer by depicting them with the shared features I have described. I have selected the Game Pass painting for detailed discussion because it is particularly explicit, but it is by no means unique. Once the behavioural characteristics of dying eland are known, it becomes immediately apparent that the juxta-25, 93, 108 positioning of medicine men with this antelope is one of the major themes of Bushman art: it is painted in a variety of ways in shelter after shelter in the south-eastern mountains and even in the rock engravings it is a prominent theme.

By using the nineteenth-century ethnography, reports from the Kalahari and the art itself we have now been able to isolate a key concept in Bushman art and thought and so reach the threshold of understanding what the artists were actually accomplishing. At a very simple level, one could argue that the artists were merely comparing the trancing medicine man with a dying eland. The painting is then no more than a simile which says A is like B. But what would be the point of the supposed comparison? Would it be merely descriptive or, perhaps, simply an aesthetic embellishment? There is obviously far more to the painting than that; aesthetics in no ways accounts for the impact of the painting. We should rather see the metaphor as the *interaction* between two elements, the medicine man and the eland.

To analyse this interaction we must first reconstruct the system of associations acquired by the eland in Bushman thought, that is, the whole range of ideas about, and responses to, the animal. Such a system of associations is, of course, culturally controlled. Our response to an animal will not necessarily be the same as the Bushman response. In fact, 'eland' is not a very resonant word to our way of thinking; it is certainly not as rich as our words 'lion', 'wolf' or 'vulture', the metaphorical uses of which are familiar to us all. So, if we wish to understand the eland metaphor as interaction, we must derive from the Bushmen themselves what their eland system of associations is.

This chapter and the preceding chapters have provided a glimpse, but only a glimpse, of the very complex associations of the eland in Bushman thought. In addition to 'dying', other postures and associations point to further segments of the eland's rich range of meaning. I can refer to these extensions of the eland symbol only briefly. The eland acquired some of its associations from three rites of passage: girls' puberty observances, boys' first-kill rituals and marriage. In the girls' puberty rituals male and female dancers mimed eland mating behaviour; the boys' first-kill observances required the shooting of an eland and the use of its fat in scarification; and in marriage the bride was anointed with eland fat. Although trance performance was the most important association of eland, it was by no means the only one.

None of these ritual associations is part of our own set of ideas about the eland; we feel little of the animal's power or richness. In paintings which juxtapose or conflate dying eland and 'dying' medicine men the artist was taking the complex Bushman system of eland associations and making it 'fit' a man in trance. His viewers were thus led, by the eland system of associations, to

51

construct a corresponding system for the man. Those human traits that could, as it were, be spoken of in 'eland language' were rendered prominent, while those that could not were suppressed. Some of the human traits indeed might not have been expressible at all except in 'eland language'; the eland system filtered them out and highlighted them. The medicine man was thus transfigured by the metaphor.

Although it was, of course, men who applied the eland system of associations to themselves to say something about themselves, we must recognise that, in the process, the eland system itself was altered. This is the interaction: the man became more eland-like, and the eland became more man-like. The eland system of associations was itself enriched by the two-way process of the metaphor.

Such interaction, which is the essence of paintings such as the one at Game Pass, cannot be reduced to literal statements like 'The trancing man trembles like a dying eland', or 'The trancing man sweats like a dying eland' and so on. Reduction involves a real loss of meaning. The metaphor is not just a matter of elegance or decoration which can be discarded without seriously altering the statement. The paraphrase fails to give the insight or the same information that the painted metaphor does. Certainly, it loses the power to arrest attention. The painting holds before its viewers the two systems of associations, the eland's and the man's, allows them to interact in the mind of the individual viewer, and produces out of that interaction a new, potent and irreducible statement. The painting creates meaning. It is a statement in its own right.

But metaphor is more than subtle meaning and the creation of meaning; it actually *does* things.

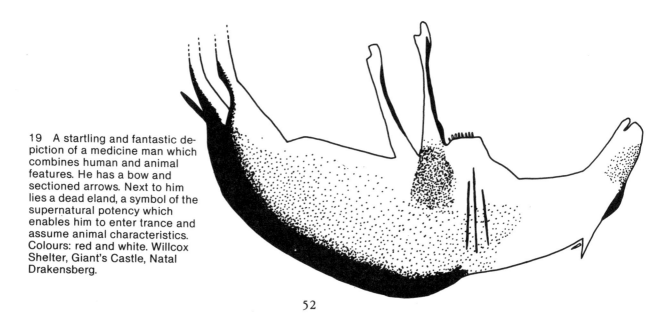

19 A startling and fantastic depiction of a medicine man which combines human and animal features. He has a bow and sectioned arrows. Next to him lies a dead eland, a symbol of the supernatural potency which enables him to enter trance and assume animal characteristics. Colours: red and white. Willcox Shelter, Giant's Castle, Natal Drakensberg.

Men resort to animal metaphors to change themselves. Each new painting with its own subtle variations added new power to the Bushmen's concept of the medicine man. In this sense, we may say that the artists played an important role in controlling the people's response to the powers of the medicine men. Furthermore, if the artists were themselves medicine men, they were actually strengthening themselves by painting the depictions I have described. All the paintings of the dying man–eland in some way imbued the medicine men with eland-potency. Their whole being merged with the most powerful of all creatures.

I have now traced the metaphor of the dying eland from myth, through ritual to the art. In the

myth, the carnivorous meerkats killed and then appropriated the potency of the Mantis's eland. Not even the eland's creator was able to fight successfully against the eland's power; his arrows flew back at him, and he returned home defeated. In ritual, Bushman hunters still dance 'eland potency' next to an eland carcass; by harnessing its potency they are able to enter the 'half death' of trance where, like the meerkats, they successfully deflect the mystical 'arrows of sickness' which always threaten them. Finally, the painters, with their understanding of the creative relationship between death and power, graphically superimposed the eland's associations on the medicine men to make a subtle and complex statement about their central religious ritual. All three contexts – myth, ritual and art – were thus linked by metaphor: the eland was a unifying thread running through Bushman belief and ritual.

I have concentrated on the eland because it is the most frequently painted metaphor and because we have the most detailed ethnography on its meaning. It was, however, by no means the only animal which had symbolic value for the Bushmen. A particularly interesting painting at Giant's Castle combines the symbolism of eland and felines. It shows a dead eland lying on its back next to a bizarre figure which seems to incorporate some feline features: it has paws and whiskers, although the ears are distinctly not feline. This combination can be explained by further beliefs about trance. When a man's spirit left his body on out-of-body travel, it frequently did so in the form of a lion. Some of Bleek's nineteenth-century informants described such adventures, one of which ended in tragedy when the medicine man in feline form killed a farmer's ox and was shot by the enraged owner. In the Kalahari today the Bushmen call felines *jummi*, 'pawed creatures', and use the same word as a verb to mean 'to go on out-of-body travel in the form of a lion'. Paintings of feline medicine men are comparatively rare because the lion seems to have symbolised the 'wild', anti-social possibilities of trance, while the antelope form suggested the beneficial accomplishments of medicine men.

This feline medicine man with his dead eland comes from the south-eastern mountains of Region III. The artists of other areas emphasised different animals (see Chapter Three). A variety of factors probably governed the selection of these particular animals as symbols: without any ethnography to guide us we can only speculate why the artists of the south-western Cape were so interested in elephant or the Zimbabwean painters in kudu and giraffe. Whatever tho e factors might have been, some quite detailed features of the art are found all over southern Africa and suggest that the animals painted in the different regions carried a broadly similar symbolic load. The supine therianthrope and juxtaposed animals at Diana's Vow, for example, can probably be interpreted in terms of the concepts I have outlined in this chapter.

Throughout southern Africa the various painted or engraved animals were complex metaphors, not just aesthetically pleasing depictions. By the artists' alchemy the animal metaphors crystallised on the walls of the rock shelters, each facet reflecting a different segment of their complex semantic spectrum.

CHAPTER SIX

Reading rock art

In the previous chapter I considered some of the metaphorical principles behind Bushman art. Now I use these principles to show that what often appears to be a confused array of unrelated paintings is, in fact, a conceptual unity constructed according to certain conventions.

It has often been assumed that, in painting such dense panels, the Bushman artists ignored the work of their predecessors and so painted next to and even over other paintings without intending any relationship between their work and that already on the walls of the shelter. I believe this is a mistaken impression which arises from two factors. First, the western viewer is used to an art of 'framed' compositions, but on the walls of the rock shelters the groups appear to grade into one another, and it is often impossible to be sure to which a given painting belongs. Only if we can put aside the western notions of framed compositions and scenic relationships, can we begin to appreciate the complexity of these large reticular panels. The question of where groups begin and end is relatively unimportant: the panel is rather a network of relationships.

The second reason why it is often thought that the painted panel is a confused collection of discrete paintings is that western viewers are unfamiliar with Bushman symbols and metaphors such as those I discussed in Chapter Five. Once these symbols and metaphors are understood, it becomes clear that successive generations of artists were commenting on, refining and explicating the ideas which they found when they came to add their own contribution. In painting his own work the artist was participating in a continuing tradition rather than creating individual *objets d'art*.

The ways in which the Bushmen achieved this developmental art are also largely unfamiliar to westerners. Some of the units of the art are, it is true, easily identifiable as activity or narrative groups; these depict such events as dances, hunts, cattle raids or domestic scenes. But sometimes there are other paintings next to and even in the midst of these activity groups which appear to be quite irrelevant. An eland, for example, might be placed next to a domestic group. The relationship is then clearly not scenic; the painter was not portraying an antelope walking past a camp. On the contrary, I argue that these paintings are intentionally juxtaposed to relate the symbolic associations of one representation to another. Such intentional juxtapositioning is not as alien to westerners as one might think: advertisers sometimes juxtapose their product with people or items which are intended to create a desirable social ambience.

Superpositioning, on the other hand, is more puzzling. Sometimes three and four layers of paintings can be discerned. As I explained in Chapter Four, quantitative analyses of the subjects involved has revealed some of the rules which governed the construction of superpositions, but, again, it is an appreciation of the symbolic associations of those subjects that unravels the apparent confusion.

The two paintings which I interpret in detail in this chapter show that it is metaphorical relationships which link both juxtaposed and superimposed paintings. I start with a painting that is now preserved in the South African Museum, Cape Town; it was removed from a southern Drakensberg shelter at the beginning of this century.

The oldest part of the painting is the somewhat faded eland. Its lowered head and stumbling posture suggest that, like so many other comparable paintings, it is dying. Death is also implied by the arrow or spear protruding from its back. The dying eland, as I showed in Chapter Five, is a major symbol in Bushman art. Principally, it is analogous to the 'dying' medicine man who, by his 'death', enters trance to protect all members of the band from whatever evil may be threatening them.

This dying eland was painted first; it is also the central theme which the same artist, or more probably subsequent artists, elaborated by juxtaposing further paintings. On the left are two imposing therianthropes with distinct eland heads and human legs. Their humanity is further implied by the long skin cloak or kaross worn by the one on the extreme left. The kaross, however, grades into the shape of an eland's distinctive hump. Numerous therianthropes have similar humps, and they have been mistaken for bundles being carried by men beneath their

20 Therianthropes, birds, baboon and men juxtaposed with a dying eland. Colours: red and white. Cala, eastern Cape.

56

karosses, but this painting shows quite clearly that at least some of the bulges have been painted to suggest the characteristic shape of an eland's back: what is an animal skin cloak at one extreme is part of the eland's body at the other.

The meaning of the fusion of man and animal in this humped, kaross-clad figure is clarified by a feature common to both therianthropes (figures combining animal and human features): they are bleeding from the nose as if they were medicine men in trance. They are, in fact, another example of the imaginative combination of man and antelope to imply the exploitation of eland-power by trancing medicine men. Trance is also suggested by the projection from the back of the neck of the right-hand figure. It is from this very spot that the Kalahari medicine men say they eject the sickness or evil they have drawn out of their patients; with a high-pitched scream and a convulsive, hunching movement the sickness is expelled and banished from the camp. As it leaves the nape of the man's neck it can be seen by other men in trance. Some medicine men are painted with far more elaborate, trailing streamers which are sometimes a development of the comparatively simple form in this painting. The same therianthrope has two lines emerging from the top of its eland head. Although these might at first glance be mistaken for horns, they are pointing in the wrong direction; eland horns slope back in line with the forehead and are not at right angles to the forehead as these lines are. It seems more likely that the lines represent the departing spirit, for it is from the top of the head that a man's spirit is said to go on out-of-body travel. This is another event which can be seen only by men in trance. Numerous other depictions of trancing medicine men have similar lines leaving the top of the head.

A less easily explained feature is the 'tusk' on the snout of the figure to the left. Like the lines

21 Medicine men who have fallen to their knees in trance and whose departing spirits are represented by lines emanating from the tops of their heads. A also bleeds from the nose, while B has an antelope head with horns. The line from the back of B's neck probably depicts the expulsion of evil and sickness. See Chapters Five and Six for a more detailed explanation of the beliefs depicted in such paintings. Colours: red and white. A: Balloch, Barkly East, B: Cullen's Wood, Barkly East.

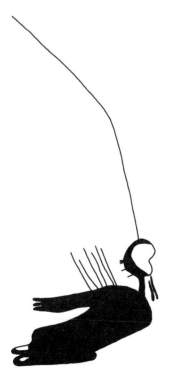

A

B

22 Large-shouldered therianthropes with 'tusks'. They have been juxtaposed with a dying eland. Colours: red and white. Game Pass, Kamberg, Natal Drakensberg.

from the top of the head, such 'tusks' are also frequently painted on therianthropes, but at Qacha's Nek there are two intertwined serpents with what appear to be antelope heads and ears and also large, distinct 'tusks'. Although we cannot at present say just what the 'tusk' represents, it seems possible that it is an expression of another, as yet unknown, belief about trance.

The second eland-man from the left is associated with a more distinctly human figure which holds an object to the therianthrope's nose. This peculiar relationship is repeated in some comparable paintings in which a man reaches out to the nose of an eland. Two aspects of Bushman beliefs about 'control' seem to be expressed in these paintings. In the case of the therianthrope we are considering, it is the depth or degree of his trance state that is being controlled. A medicine man strives to control the level of his trance so that he does not go into a violent or cataleptic state. This extreme condition was, and still is, considered dangerous and undesirable. To stave off the violent throes of trance a man was sometimes cared for by being given aromatic herbs called *buchu* to smell. The power in the scent of the buchu enabled him to maintain the desired level of trance in which he could still move around to cure the people. It therefore seems probable that the object being held to the therianthrope's nose is the calming or restraining buchu.

The second aspect of control that is probably also expressed here is the control of animals. As I explained in Chapter Two, medicine men of the game were believed to control antelope as medicine men of the rain were able to control the movements of the rain-animal. If the rain-animal proved intractable or dangerously wild, it could be calmed by being given sweet-smelling

23 A man reaches out to an eland's nose. This painting probably depicts the medicine man's ability to control antelope. The hartebeest (lower right) was, like the eland, considered to possess much supernatural potency. The man below the eland is in the bending-forward posture adopted by trance dancers. Scale in centimetres. Colours: red and white. Fulton's Rock, Giant's Castle, Natal Drakensberg.

buchu which it loved. The paintings of a man holding out an object to an eland's nose might therefore be showing a similar circumstance in which a medicine man is using buchu to control the movements, not of a rain-animal, but of an otherwise unmanageable antelope. One such painting in the Natal Drakensberg also shows white dots falling from the man's armpits; these might represent the sweat of trance. Close by is another, less well-preserved man wearing one of the caps with antelope ears which were believed to help control the movements of antelope. His cap is therefore communicating the same idea as the man reaching out to the eland's nose.

These two aspects of control may be simultaneously present in the painting of the man holding out something to the nose of the therianthrope. Such eland–men are, in a metaphorical sense, both medicine men *and* dying eland. They are exploiting the potency of the dying eland to secure the death of further eland. As the wild antelope must be controlled, so the 'wild' behaviour of the trancing man must also be controlled by the application of potent, aromatic buchu. The human figure is therefore controlling both the death of eland and the level of a medicine man's trance. The artist has imaginatively expressed the ambiguities in beliefs about trance by skilfully manipulating a series of metaphors.

In contrast to this highly complex, metaphorical section of the painting is a single, partially preserved human figure near the eland's head. Fortunately, enough of this figure has been preserved to show that it is a man in the arms-back posture which is adopted by medicine men when they are intensifying their dancing to enter trance. This single dancer is, then, a literal

59

depiction of the beliefs which are far more subtly dealt with by the metaphorical figures to the left. Perhaps it was added as a more explicit gloss on the other paintings.

So far I have avoided commenting on what must seem the most extraneous paintings in the group, the baboon and the two birds. Far from being irrelevant they are a further development in the network of meanings which the artist (or artists) has drawn out of the original, dying eland. The kneeling posture of the baboon recalls the position to which trance dancers sometimes fall when they enter trance; but more significant are the lines on the baboon's face. Similar red lines are frequently drawn across the faces of medicine men and even some eland. It seems very probable that these lines are not scarification marks, as has been supposed, but a stylised representation of the nasal blood of trance. Furthermore, the southern Bushmen saw their dances as comparable with baboons' antics and believed that it was a baboon who taught the people the medicine songs. According to a Bushman legend these potent songs were originally the possessions of the baboon, the lion and the ostrich, but the lion fought the ostrich, and, as a result of this deplorable strife, the songs left them and they all became animals. The possession of the medicine songs is thus one of the factors which distinguish men from animals: man's mastery, in the trance dance, of the songs' supernatural potency separates him from the natural world. These Bushman beliefs show that the painted baboon refers to further aspects of trance; it is by no means an irrelevant or discrete depiction.

With the baboon we are on fairly safe ground because there are clear statements by southern Bushman informants which show that it was part of the whole set of trance beliefs. The birds, however, cannot be as easily explained because there are no ethnographic references to beliefs about them. Nevertheless, we can hazard an intelligent guess if we bear in mind that animals are often selected for symbolic purposes because of some feature of their behaviour. The dying eland

24 Three medicine men who have fallen to their knees in trance. The one on the left has antelope hoofs in place of feet and his arms are in the 'flying' posture. The man on the right has his arms in the backward posture adopted by a man asking God for potency. Colours: red and white. Burley II, Barkly East.

60

and the gambolling baboons are two examples which we have already noted. Although the shape of the birds' bodies could suggest guinea fowl, the dark band around the neck is a very distinctive feature of the Egyptian Goose. If this identification of the bird is correct, its appropriateness in this painting is readily explained. The Egyptian Goose is a bird which inhabits both water and the air: it can move from one realm to the other. Similarly, the medicine men were thought to inhabit the same two realms. In trance a man could 'fly' on out-of-body travel, a metaphor still used in the Kalahari where some Bushmen call the bending-forward, arms-outstretched dancing posture 'flying'. While flying is one metaphor for trance, being under water is, as I explained in Chapter Five, another. As the medicine man inhabits both water and sky, so too does the Egyptian Goose. Its depiction here may, therefore, be seen as a further, reinforcing metaphor which refers to the medicine man's ability to transcend natural restrictions and to inhabit different worlds.

All the features and associations to which I have now drawn attention show that, far from being a jumble of unrelated paintings, this group has been carefully constructed according to certain metaphorical conventions to develop ideas implicit in the first painted representation, the dying eland. In addition to those conventions there is a painted feature which visually and more explicitly links the paintings. It is the red line, sometimes fringed with white dots, which appears at numerous sites. Here it joins the therianthropes, and, in another section, runs from one of the birds to the back of the dying eland's neck, the same area from which the medicine man expels sickness. A third section, without the white dots, joins the other bird to the baboon. These lines confirm my argument that some juxtaposed but apparently unrelated paintings are often part of the same composition.

There is, however, no western concept which can explain the meaning of this curious linear feature. Fortunately, the nineteenth-century Bushman ethnography preserves details of a set of beliefs which explain the line in its various forms. These beliefs all relate to aspects of the supernatural potency to which I have had occasion to refer again and again. Those paintings which show the line at the feet of dancers probably represent the potency which their dancing is activating; those which show men running along the line probably depict men on out-of-body travel being sustained in that dangerous state by their potency. In other cases, such as the one linking the two therianthropes, the line probably represents potency passing between trancing medicine men. As the men dance, or while they are exhausted in trance, they hold one another to facilitate the passage of potency between them. This interaction helps to protect them while they are in the perilous 'half death' of trance. Similarly, the lines linking the bird to the eland and the second bird to the baboon probably represent, even more symbolically, the passage of potency between trance dancers: the medicine men are here no longer depicted in anything like human form, but by symbols of the trance state.

The whole composition can, then, be seen as juxtaposed symbols all related to the central idea of trance. Each new addition to the group brought out further subtleties implicit in the original dying eland. The principle linking all the depictions is symbolic juxtapositioning. The second linking principle, superpositioning, is illustrated in another painting, this time from the eastern Drakensberg. The black and white copy here has been redrawn (and slightly simplified) from Harald Pager's photograph of the original painting published in his book *Ndedema*.

In this elegant composition a group of eland has been superimposed on three elongated human figures. Two of these figures carry hunting bags and all three have bows and arrows. The arrows have been painted in such great detail that it is possible to distinguish between those with slender bone points and those with the broader iron points. Each hunter appears to be wearing a cap with one or two 'flaps' hanging down at the back. Their heads are of the 'hooked' type, the white face being preserved on the first two from the left. The Bushman artists tended to use human figures with this kind of conventionalised head in superpositioning more frequently than figures with less complex head types, despite there being a marked overall preponderance of the simpler forms.

7, 21–4 Moreover, the frequent appearance of the white-face type in ritual groups suggests that the white face is yet another, but imperfectly understood, indicator of trance performance. If this is indeed so, and numerous paintings point to this conclusion, the elongation of these and so many other human figures might be an attempt to depict the rising sensation of trance about which medicine men speak. The three hunters depicted here might thus be medicine men of the game in trance.

Whether or not I am correct in believing that these are medicine men, there can be no doubt whatsoever that they are hunters with all their hunting equipment. Neither can there be any doubt that viewers were intended to discern a relationship between the hunters and the group of eland. This is a case in which the uniform preservation of the paintings suggests that no great time lapse occurred between the painting of the men and the antelope. Furthermore, there is clean rock surface nearby on which the eland could have been painted if the artist had wished to keep them separate from the men. If there is indeed the intended relationship I suspect, what does it mean? To answer that question we must examine the grouping and postures of the eland in more detail.

This and the previous chapter will have equipped the reader to identify without much difficulty
59, 93 the dying eland on the right: its staggering, head-down posture is very similar to others I have described and illustrated. Furthermore, there is possibly the important two-way relationship between it and the hunters. If, as I argue, the hunters are also medicine men of the game, they are probably intentionally related to the released potency of the superimposed, dying eland so that, by harnessing that potency in trance, they can secure the death of eland which they and their fellows will hunt in the future.

This composition is not, however, restricted to the death of eland: eland mating is also implied. The broad neck of the dying eland indicates that it is a bull eland. The sex of the upper recumbent eland, is, because of its posture, more difficult to identify, but the central, recumbent eland and the one viewed from the rear are both females. The association of males and females in the same herd is, as Kalahari Bushmen pointed out to me, a seasonal feature indicative of mating. At other times of the year the cows and bulls split up into smaller, single-sex herds. Mating is still more explicitly suggested by the remarkable end-on eland. Eland, like many other animals, flick their tails to keep off flies; in this movement the tail swings around the flanks so that the terminal tuft seldom rises far above the level of the back. In the mating behaviour of this antelope, however, the female first flicks her tail violently from side to side as the male approaches her, and then, when the male mounts, she raises her tail and assumes the posture depicted.

Such eland mating behaviour is mimed by male and female dancers in the important girls' puberty rituals. The Eland Bull dance, as it is called, is performed around a small hut in which the girl is secluded. The women, having removed their aprons and having put on 'tails' of ostrich eggshell beads, mime the heavy, swaying gait of eland cows. The one or two older men who have fixed eland horns or blackened sticks to their heads approach the women. The dance is

25 A group of eland superimposed on elongated human figures. The postures of the eland suggest symbolic meanings. The men are carrying slender bone-pointed arrows and broader iron-pointed arrows. Scale in centimetres. Colours: red and white. Botha's Shelter, Ndedema Gorge, Natal Drakensberg.

accompanied by the clicking of metal knives to suggest the very characteristic clicking sound made by an eland's hoofs as it walks, and by the singing of the ancient Great Eland Song. The whole performance is considered so intensely beautiful that the girl in seclusion is moved to tears. At the height of the dance, some Bushmen say, an eland approaches the camp; the people are fearful, but the old men reassure them that it is a good thing come from God.

There is a great deal more to these girls' puberty rituals, but for the present we must simply note that they are performed not merely to mark the attainment of adult status and eligibility for marriage, but also to ensure the well-being of the whole camp. The eland rituals are believed to secure adequate rainfall and good hunting. If certain observances are omitted, the eland, they say, will become wild and escape the hunters.

The resonances of the eland mating herd in this painting are therefore extensive and subtle. Eland mating communicates ideas of maturity, good hunting, adequate rainfall and the safety of all members of the camp. These are also some of the ends to which the medicine men strive in trance. Eland mating, in fact, complements the symbolism of the dying eland. It would, therefore, be wrong to say that a painting like this can be decoded to give a simple, straightforward message such as 'These men are hunting eland.' On the contrary, the artist superimposed symbols so that their complex associations could interact in the minds of the viewers; each painter was able, by his own genius, to participate in the continuing exploration of recondite beliefs, and each viewer could trace the network of implied meanings. The essential unity within the complexity of Bushman thought has been marvellously caught by the artists; what they said in a few juxtaposed or superimposed depictions has required many pages of explanation.

Not all paintings are, of course, as complex as these two: sometimes a shelter may contain only a couple of standing eland. These 'simpler' paintings are, paradoxically, more difficult to explain; certainly, it is impossible to say with any confidence that a single aspect of eland symbolism was being emphasised. It seems more likely that, in these cases, all the manifold resonances of the eland were present awaiting explication by future artists who never came. The ancient tradition in which generations of artists had participated for millennia ended abruptly and tragically. We shall never know what further aesthetic achievements and symbolic subtleties would have graced the rocks of southern Africa.

CHAPTER SEVEN

The end of a tradition

From the moment the Dutch established a permanent settlement at the Cape of Good Hope, the Bushmen were a condemned people.

For well over a thousand years the hunters had lived alongside the pastoral Hottentots in the west and the agricultural Bantu-speakers in the east. During this extended period there were no doubt clashes, particularly in the early decades, but it seems that the different groups settled down to a reasonably amicable coexistence. In many cases the Bushmen entered into a mutually beneficial client relationship with the newcomers. The Bushmen hunted and collected firewood for the agriculturalists; for their part, the Bantu-speakers respected the Bushmen's accomplishments in magical affairs and employed them to perform rain-making ceremonies. In more recent times at any rate, some Bushman families lived permanently with the Bantu-speakers so that they would be on hand to conduct rituals.

But the symbiosis of these earlier centuries was disturbed and finally destroyed when the new element was introduced at the Cape. As the Dutch settlement expanded into the interior and along the southern coast, the Hottentot herders were the first to experience the social disintegration brought about by the new value placed on cattle and the loss of their ancestral grazing land. Then the Bushman groups of the Cape Colony came under pressure, and, finally, when the white advance had been halted on the eastern frontier by the black farmers, the Bushmen of the south-eastern mountains found it increasingly difficult to maintain the old hunter–gatherer economy.

One of the stereotypes of southern African history has been to present the Bushmen of this turbulent period as a helpless people unable to cope with changing circumstances. This is not entirely true: they responded in a variety of ways to the new factors. Some took to herding cattle and sheep and so, in a sense, ceased to be Bushmen. Others intermarried with the Hottentots, the Bantu-speakers and the white frontiersmen. Still others tried to retain at least part of the old life by entering into pacts with the white farmers. In return for a few sheep they undertook not to raid the colonists' herds or flocks. The colonists found it difficult to negotiate these agreements because the Bushmen had no chiefs, and a truce with one camp was not binding on any others. The pacts therefore often ended disastrously for both sides. The settlers turned indiscriminately on all

Bushmen, hunting them down with appalling ferocity. Towards the end of the eighteenth century Sparrman deplored the white onslaught: 'Does a colonist at any time get view of a Boshies-man, he takes fire immediately, and spirits up his horse and dogs, in order to hunt him with more hardness and fury than he would a wolf or any other wild beast.' But the agreements were doomed for another reason as well: the farmers were insatiably land-hungry and constantly extending the frontier. The Dutch argued that because the Bushmen did not pasture cattle or cultivate the soil, they were worthless vagabonds wasting valuable resources and they would be better off working for the whites. Poverty, cruelty and disease were all too often the lot of those Bushmen who accepted this alternative.

Others understandably preferred to cling to the old way of life. Barrow himself described the terrible suffering of some groups in the eastern Cape who were forced to remain in the mountains throughout the harsh, cold winters. Plant foods were scarce and antelope few: their only course was to raid the whites who occupied the milder plains. George Stow, who wrote in the second half of the nineteenth century, described how some similarly placed camps tried, in the face of great danger, to maintain their old annual, seasonal round and so visited and revisited the caves in which their artists had for centuries painted.

It is not known exactly when or how the last artist died. Stow was told how a man said to be the 'last known Bushman artist of the Malutis' was shot while on a marauding expedition to capture some horses. He was reported to have had ten small horn pots hanging from a belt, each of which contained a different paint. Perhaps painting was one of the important parts of their disintegrating culture, one to which some of the final southern Bushmen clung tenaciously. For those who chose to remain in the mountains the art must have spoken of an idyllic past imbued with eland-power. When Stow showed some copies he had made of rock paintings to an old Bushman couple, they at once identified the dances therein depicted. On seeing one of these, the old woman began to sing and dance. Her husband was so moved that he begged her to desist. 'Don't', he said, 'don't sing those old songs, I can't bear it! It makes my heart too sad!' She, however, persisted, and finally, the old man joined her. They looked at one another, Stow wrote, and were happy, the glance of the wife seeming to say, 'Ah! I thought you could not withstand *that*!'

That poignant incident took place over a century ago. Now the southern Bushmen are extinct and even their art is slowly vanishing. We owe a tremendous debt to Stow, Wilhelm Bleek and those few early writers who preserved enough of the Bushman's beliefs to enable us to attain the degree of understanding I have described in this book. As Bleek himself realised, the rock paintings are not 'the mere daubing of figures for idle pastime' but an astonishing expression of those 'ideas which most deeply moved the Bushman mind, and filled it with religious feelings'.

A short bibliography

CHAPTER I

Fock, G. J. 1979. *Felsbilder in Sudafrika, Teil I.* Köln: Böhlau Verlag.

Lewis-Williams, J. D. 1981. *Believing and seeing: symbolic meanings in southern San rock paintings.* London: Academic Press.

  1983. *New approaches to southern African rock art.* Goodwin Series 4. Cape Town: South African Archaeological Society.

Pager, H. 1971. *Ndedema.* Graz: Akademische Druck Verlagsanstalt.

Vinnicombe, P. 1976. *People of the Eland.* Pietermaritzburg: Natal University Press.

Willcox, A. R. 1963. *The rock art of South Africa.* London: Nelson.

CHAPTER II

Lee, R. B. 1979. *The !Kung San: men, women and work in a foraging society.* Cambridge: Cambridge University Press.

Marshall, L. 1976. *The !Kung of Nyae Nyae.* Cambridge, Mass.: Harvard University Press.

Rudner, I. 1982. Khoisan pigments and paints and their relationship to rock paintings. *Ann. S. Afr. Mus.* 87:1–281.

Silberbauer, G. B. 1981. *Hunter and habitat in the central Kalahari desert.* Cambridge: Cambridge University Press.

Tobias, P. V. (ed.) 1978. *The Bushmen.* Cape Town: Human and Rousseau.

CHAPTER III

Butzer, K. W., Fock, G. J., Scott, L. and Stuckenrath, R. 1979. Dating and context of rock engravings in southern Africa. *Science* 203: 1201–14.

Deacon, J. H., Deacon, J. and Brooker, M. 1976. Four painted stones from Boomplaas Cave, Oudtshoorn district. *S. Afr. Archaeol. Bull.,* 31: 141–5

Thackeray, A. I., Thackeray, J. F., Beaumont, P. B. and Vogel, J. C. 1981. Dated rock engravings from Wonderwerk Cave, South Africa. *Science* 214: 64–7.

Wendt, W. E. 1974. 'Art mobilier' aus der Apollo 11-Grotte in Südwest-Afrika. *Acta Praehistorica et Archaeologica* 5: 1–42.

CHAPTER IV

Lewis-Williams, J. D. 1972. The syntax and function of the Giant's Castle rock paintings. *S. Afr. Archaeol. Bull.* 27: 49–65.

  1974. Superpositioning in a sample of rock-paintings from the Barkly East district. *S. Afr. Archaeol. Bull.* 29: 93–103.

Maggs, T. M. O'C. 1967. A quantitative analysis of the rock art from a sample area in the western Cape. *S. Afr. Journ. Sci.* 63 (3):100–4.

Vinnicombe, P. 1967. Rock painting analysis. *S. Afr. Archaeol. Bull.* 22: 129–41.

  1972. Myth, motive, and selection in southern African rock art. *Africa* 42 (3): 192–204.

CHAPTER V

Biesele, M. 1978. Sapience and scarce resources: communication systems of the !Kung and other foragers. *Soc. Sci. Info.* 17:921–47.

Bleek, D. F. 1924. *The Mantis and his friends.* Cape Town: Maskew Millar.

Bleek, W. H. I. and Lloyd, L. C. 1911. *Specimens of Bushman folklore.* London: Allen.

Lewis-Williams, J. D. 1982. The social and economic context of southern San rock art. *Current Anthropology*, 23: 429–49.

CHAPTER VI

Lewis-Williams, J. D. 1977. Ezeljagdspoort revisited: new light on an enigmatic rock painting. *S. Afr. Archaeol. Bull.* 32:165–9.

1980. Ethnography and iconography: aspects of southern San thought and art. *Man* 15:467–82.

1981. The thin red line: southern San notions and rock paintings of supernatural potency. *S. Afr. Archaeol. Bull.* 36:5–13.

Vinnicomb, P. 1975. The ritual significance of eland (*Taurotragus oryx*) in the rock art of southern Africa. In Anati, E. (ed.) *Les Religions de la Préhistoire.* Capo di Ponte: Centro Preistorici.

CHAPTER VII

Inskeep, R. R. 1978. *The peopling of southern Africa.* London: David Philip.

Wilson, M. and Thompson, L. 1969. *The Oxford history of South Africa.* Oxford: Oxford University Press.

ACKNOWLEDGEMENTS

The following people and institutions kindly provided illustrative material for this book: 1, 13 Mr P. Stickler; 2, 8 Mrs Lorna Marshall; 3 Dr T. M. O'C. Maggs; 4 Mr P. den Hoed; 5, 48–50, 56 Mr J. H. N. Loubser; 7 Academic Press, London; 9 Professor R. J. Mason and Witwatersrand University Press; 10 Mr F. Thackeray and *Science*; 11, 12 Dr G. H. Fock; 26–8, 30 Mr P. Moore; 32 Dr T. Volman; 29, 31, 33 Professor T. N. Huffman; 34–41 Mr N. Coetzee; 42–3 Dr W. E. Wendt; 45 Professor H. Deacon; 70, 81–2 Mr A. Rycroft; 93–5, 97 Professor L. G. A. Smits. The South African Museum and the South African Public Library gave permission to copy material in their care. The Librarian, Jagger Library, University of Cape Town, permitted quotations from the Bleek Collection. A number of friends and colleagues made useful comments on a draft of this book: Professor W. D. Hammond-Tooke, Professor T. N. Huffman, Mr T. M. Evers and Mr M. O. V. Taylor. Mrs D. Gelling kindly typed the successive versions of the book.

26 on preceding page

26 Zimbabwean rock paintings are often found in shelters formed by piles of granite boulders. Diana's Vow, Zimbabwe.

27 Supine figure with animal head. Diana's Vow, Zimbabwe.

28 Detail from 27 shows fine detail of head and the pattern of white dots on the body of the therianthrope. Diana's Vow, Zimbabwe.

29   A densely painted area which includes a zebra and men in the bending-forward posture that is often associated with trance performance. Nswatugi, Zimbabwe.

30   A few of the many paintings associated with the therianthrope shown in 27. The creature in the centre has white lines leading from its eyes to its snout, as does the therianthrope. The lines or 'streamers' from the animal's neck suggest that it is related to beliefs about trance performance. Diana's Vow, Zimbabwe.

31   Two delicately painted giraffes. Nswatugi, Zimbabwe.

32   A domestic group performing a variety of activities. One woman appears to be grinding a vegetable food, while another places her hands on the back of a seated figure in what may be a curing ritual. A seated man may be preparing arrows. Silozwene, Zimbabwe.

33   A group of dancing men juxtaposed with some of the curious forms which some writers have suggested depict granite boulders and hills (see 26), but many certainly represent beehives. In the lower left are paintings of fish, another symbol of trance performance. Lion's Head, Zimbabwe.

34   The Brandberg, rich in painted sites, rises from the arid plains of Namibia.

35   An engraved rock in the stark, arid valley at Twyfelfontein, Namibia. Twyfelfontein is one of the richest engraved sites in southern Africa.

36   Engraved rhinoceros, giraffe, eland and other animals together with a human footprint. Twyfelfontein, Namibia.

37   Giraffe and other animals. The lion's legs end in representations of lion's spoor; its exaggerated tail also terminates in the print of a lion's paw. Twyfelfontein, Namibia.

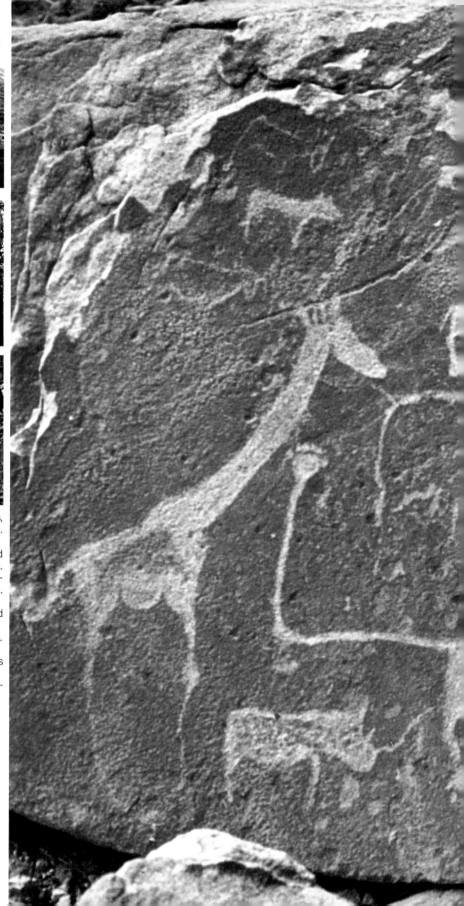

38 Detail from 39. A giraffe in white and various other paintings. Below and to the right of the white giraffe is the neck of another painted to show the chequered pattern of this animal's hide.

39 A densely painted panel in the Brandberg.

40 Eland and other antelope. Brandberg, Namibia.

41 The summer rains transform the usually dry and forbidding Brandberg.

42, 43 on following pages

42 Stone with painting of a rhinoceros excavated from the Apollo 11 shelter, southern Namibia. This and the stone in 43 have been dated by radio-carbon techniques to approximately 26 000 years B.P.

43 Two fitting fragments of stone excavated from the Apollo 11 shelter, southern Namibia. The painted animal appears to be a feline, but a pair of human legs has been added at a later date.

SOUTH-WESTERN CAPE

44 The Coldstream burial stone.
Southern Cape coast.

45 Painted stone excavated at
Boomplaas and dated to about 2000
years B.P. The painting depicts a walking
human figure with two large, enigmatic
circular marks.

46 Elephants with a hunter.
Boontjieskloof, Cedarberg, south-
western Cape.

47 Elephant surrounded by sinuous
red line. Hex River Mountains,
south-western Cape.

46, 47 on facing page, top to bottom

48 Handprints surround a large painting of an eland. The white paint has faded, leaving only the eland's body. Eland's Bay, a site which overlooks the Atlantic Ocean. South-western Cape.

49 A stylised handprint. Eland's Bay, south-western Cape.

50 A fat-tailed sheep. Eland's Bay, south-western Cape.

50 on facing page

51 A bichrome eland together with cloaked human figures. Alpha, Cedarberg, south-western Cape.

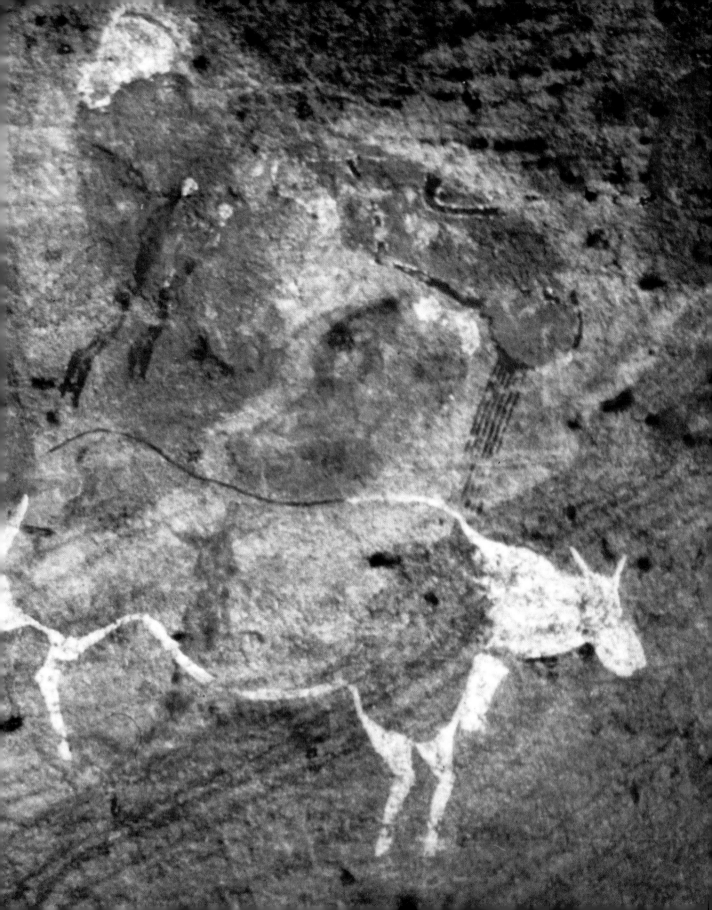

52 A supine, cloaked human figure. The head is of the 'hooked' type with a white face. Alpha, Cedarberg, south-western Cape.

53 Hartebeest and human figures. The white legs of the antelope have faded to give the appearance of disproportionately short legs. Scale in inches. Hex River Mountains, south-western Cape.

54 Elongated human figures and antelope. Alpha, Cedarberg, south-western Cape.

55 In the winter rainfall region of the south-western Cape the vegetation is much denser than in Namibia. Hex River Mountains.

56 The Alpha rock shelter. Paintings are on the overhanging rock. Cedarberg, south-western Cape.

57 The Natal Drakensberg, which reaches an altitude of 12 000 feet. In the foreground
are the flat tops of the spurs which form the Little Berg and in which most of the painted
rock shelters are found.

On following pages

59   Densely painted panel showing a dying eland with various figures. Game Pass Shelter, Kamberg, Natal Drakensberg. Scale in inches.

60   A close-up view of the therianthrope holding the tail of the dying eland in 59; its legs are crossed in imitation of the eland's crossed hind legs. The therianthrope's legs extend under the ledge of rock and terminate in carefully drawn black antelope hoofs.

61   In the centre of 59 a red figure dances in the typical bending-forward, arms-outstretched posture. The hands are white and a short cloak hangs down in front of the figure. It is superimposed on other paintings.

58   Game Pass Shelter, Kamberg, Natal Drakensberg. A large, open shelter with a commanding view. Well-preserved paintings can be seen on the wall of the shelter.

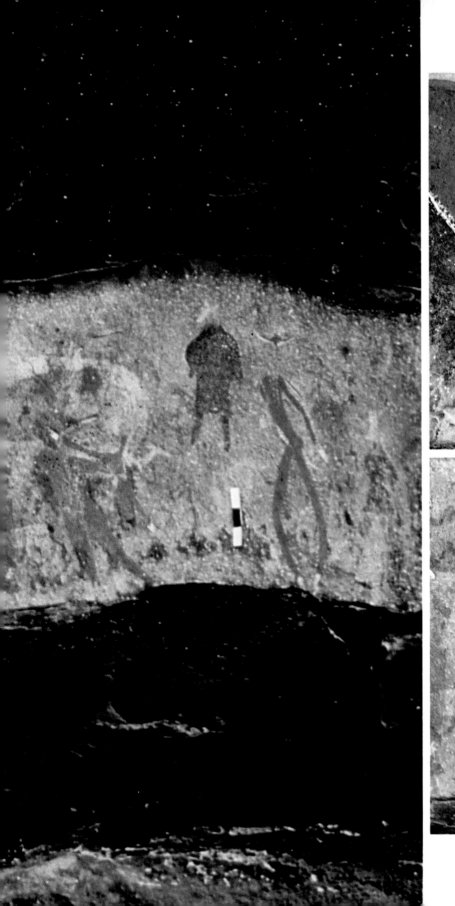

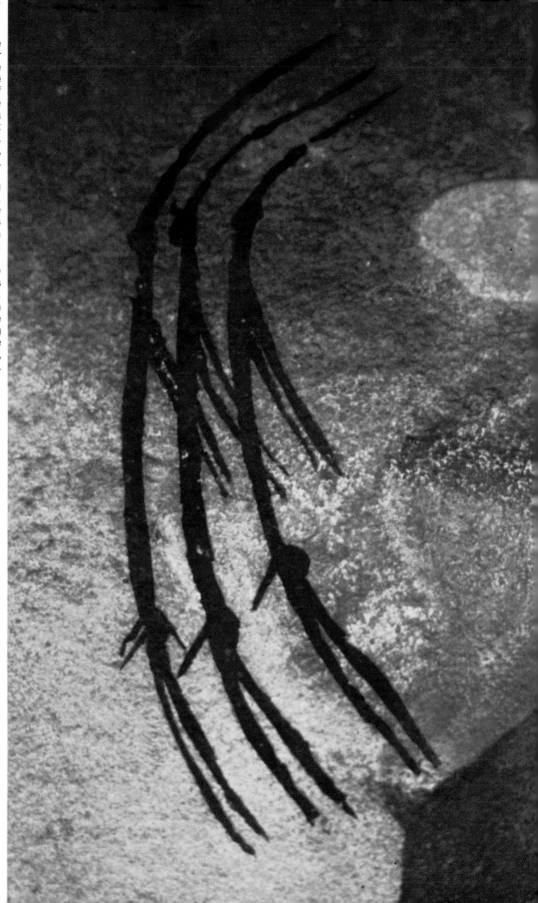

62 Close-up view of the three trance dancers in the upper left of 63. They are in the arms-back posture and have long lines from the tops of their heads which may be feather headdresses or a representation of the spirit leaving on out-of-body travel. Christmas Shelter, Kamberg, Natal Drakensberg.

63 Paintings on the ceiling of Christmas Shelter, Kamberg, Natal Drakensberg. A large eland with lowered head has been superimposed on numerous depictions.

64 A therianthropic figure with distinct human hind legs (though no feet) and buttocks. The front half is antelope in form. The artist has had more than one attempt at painting the head. Blood falls from the nose. Willem's Shelter, Kamberg, Natal Drakensberg.

65 Men dance around a hut in which a medicine man bends over a supine figure. Some figures have their hands raised as they clap the medicine songs to activate the supernatural potency which is exploited in the curing ritual. Lonyana, Kamberg, Drakensberg.

66 Line of walking figures carrying equipment; two antelope, one of which has been overpainted. The Krantzes, Kamberg, Natal Drakensberg.

66 on following pages

67 A dancing man from the Barnes's Shelter group (80). He wears two long feathers attached to a black cap.

68 Shaded polychrome therianthrope with rhebok head and wearing a white cloak. Blood falls from its nose and there is another emanation which has been mistaken for a musical instrument. Mushroom Hill, Cathedral Peak, Natal Drakensberg.

67 on facing page

69 View from Bushpig Shelter, Giant's Castle, Natal Drakensberg.

70 Fight scene. To the right a man bleeds and lies supine, while another bleeding figure leaves the conflict. In the centre a man removes an arrow from his arm. Numerous arrows are depicted amongst the combatants. Battle Cave, Injasuti, Natal Drakensberg.

71–4 on following pages, left to right

71 Bushpig. Note the way in which the artist has painted the farther ear. Bushpig Shelter, Giant's Castle, Natal Drakensberg.

72 Two baboons. Baboon Rock, Giant's Castle, Natal Drakensberg.

73 Fight scene. Central figure holds stick with bored stone. Bushpig Shelter, Giant's Castle, Natal Drakensberg.

74 Fantastic elephant with toes and elongated trunk. It is surrounded by dancing human figures and small crosses which probably represent bees. Barnes's Shelter, Giant's Castle, Natal Drakensberg.

75 Snake and elongated human figures. Main Caves, Giant's Castle, Natal Drakensberg.

76 Three large, elaborate, cloaked figures. The cloak on the right appears to be made up of a number of small skins sewn together. To the left is an eland. Upper Ncibidwane II, Giant's Castle, Natal Drakensberg.

77 Bags and quivers. Wildebeest Shelter, Giant's Castle, Natal Drakensberg.

76, 77 on facing page, top to bottom

78   Black horseman super-imposed on hindquarters of un-shaded polychrome eland. Note cloven hoofs and brush marks in thick red paint. Steel's Shelter, Giant's Castle, Natal Drakensberg.

79   Leaping horse with rider. Steel's Shelter, Giant's Castle, Natal Drakensberg.

80   Dancing, clapping and seated human figures. The line above the heads of the seated figures probably represents a rock shelter with leather bags hanging from the walls. Barnes's Shelter, Giant's Castle, Natal Drakensberg.

78, 79 on facing page,
top to bottom

81 Herd of rhebok; unshaded bichromes. Battle Cave, Injasuti, Natal Drakensberg.

82 Elongated therianthropes. Battle Cave, Injasuti, Natal Drakensberg.

83   Men on horseback hunt a herd of eland. Bellevue,
southern Drakensberg.

84 Close-up of man and horse in top left of 83. The man wears a British
soldier's uniform; his cap lies at his feet. The horse's reins are over the
man's elbow in the manner of British soldiers of the period.

85 Men on horseback pursue fleeing Bushmen; in the lower centre are cattle, the cause of the conflict. Scale in inches. Beersheba, southern Drakensberg.

86 Detail from 85. The bearded figure with broad-bladed spear is probably a Bantu-speaking servant of the white farmers.

87 Detail from 85. Dismounted man shoots at Bushmen, one of whom lies dead. Note white smoke from barrel of rifle and also the white flash from the pan. The horses' reins hang down; the Dutch settlers trained their horses to remain standing like this.

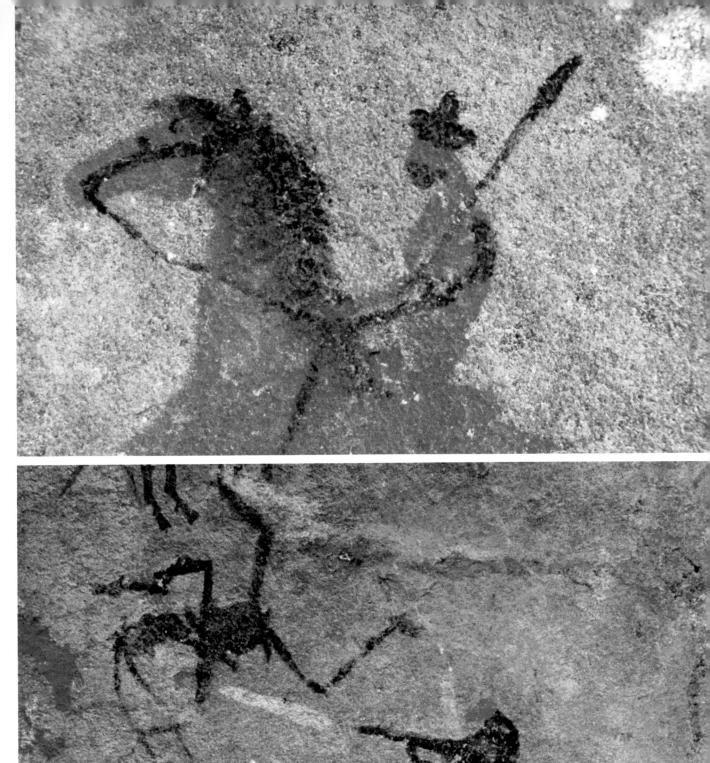

88   Animal entangled in a line which probably represents the supernatural potency controlled by medicine men of the game. Matatiele, southern Drakensberg.

89   Detail from 85. Fleeing Bushman with bows; his arrows are fixed in a fillet around his head to facilitate rapid fire.

90   Detail from 85. Horse and rider.

88, 89 on facing page, top to bottom

91   Close-up view of head of eland in lower right of 92. Note delicate shading and moulding of eye socket.

92   Shaded polychrome eland in various postures. In left centre one is viewed from above as it lies down; the dark line along an eland's back is clearly visible. Others are depicted as seen from front, rear and side. Scale in inches. The Meads, southern Drakensberg.

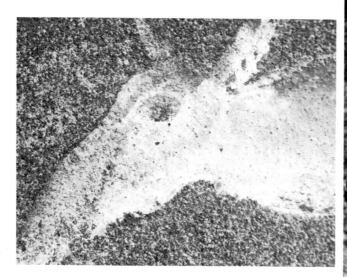

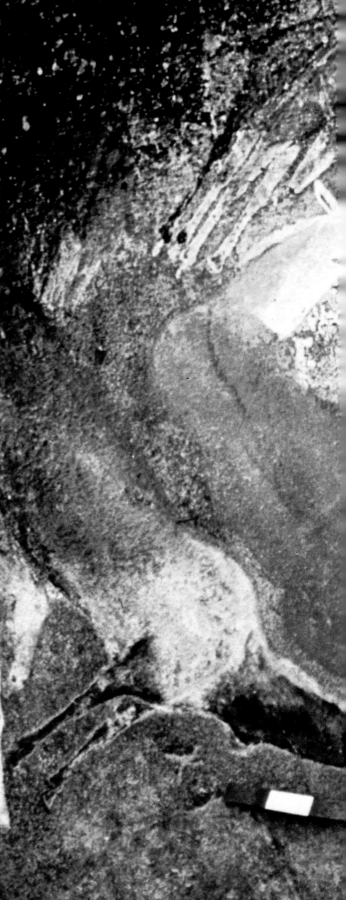

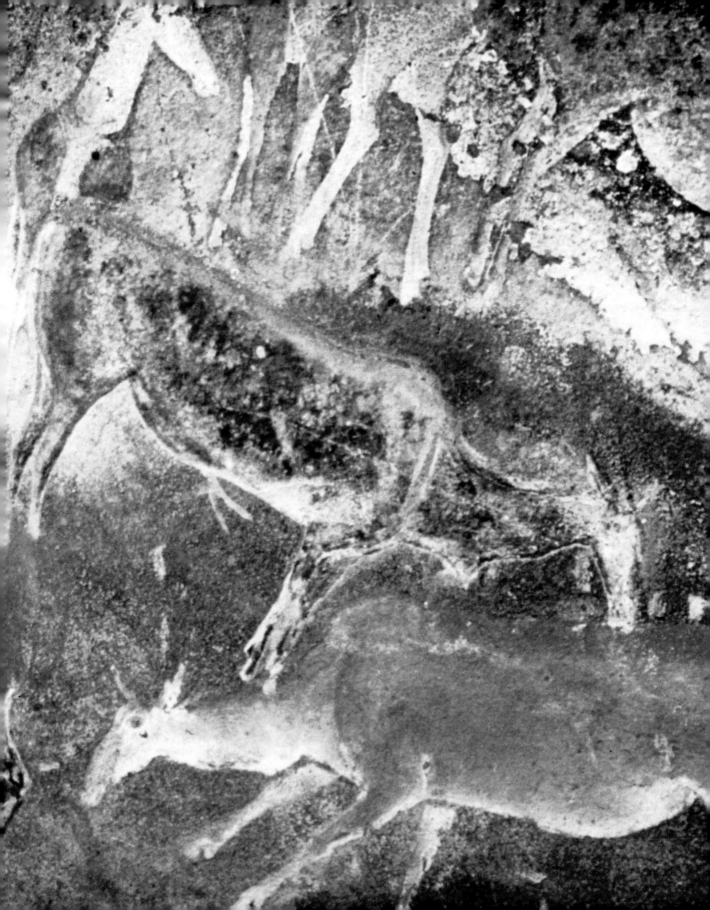

LESOTHO

93 Eland in the head-down
posture which frequently
suggests death. The very
large neck and dewlap show
that it is a bull eland.
Hermitage, Lesotho.

94   Elegantly drawn bowmen. Ha Khotso, Lesotho.

95   A pair of blue cranes. These birds migrate from the lower regions to the mountains to breed between November and February. Ha Khotso, Lesotho.

95 on facing page

96   Complex group of eland and medicine men. Leqoa
River, Lesotho.

97   Two running human figures with their legs in the
posture frequently depicted to suggest speed.
Manamolela, Lesotho.

98   Joggemspruit Valley. Fetcani Glen, a richly painted
shelter, is under the Cave Sandstone cliff on the left.
Barkly East, Eastern Cape Province.

99.   Shaded polychrome eland. Scale in inches. Fetcani
Glen, Barkly East, eastern Cape Province.

100 A man wearing dancing rattles bleeds from the nose and sags in trance. Another man, wearing a cap with antelope ears, moves in to assist him. To the right a third dancer holds a fly switch. Note elaborate details. Fetcani Bend, Barkly East, eastern Cape Province.

101 Fish. Leeufontein, eastern Cape Province. Scale in inches.

102 Eland superimposed on large therianthropes. Burley I, Barkly East, eastern Cape Province.

103 Cattle and leaping feline. Scale in inches. Buffelsfontein, eastern Cape Province.

104 Men dance, supporting their weight on two sticks, while women stand and clap rhythm. Note detail of women's fingers. Orange Springs, eastern Orange Free State.

105 Densely painted panel. The central figure is in the bending-forward dancing posture. Tripolitania, eastern Orange Free State.

106 Engraving of a rhinoceros in the classical style. Orkney, Transvaal.

107 Engraving of a hippopotamus showing detail of skin folds in the classical style. Bothaville, Orange Free State.

108 Head of an eland. Note the detail of the eye, ears, horns and folds of skin on the neck. Bothaville, Orange Free State.

104, 105 on facing page, top to bottom

109 The Natal Drakensberg at the beginning of winter when the grass has turned red. The Bushmen probably left their painted shelters at this time and moved down to the warmer plains. Giant's Castle.

109 on following pages